EAST TO CATHAY

The Silk Road

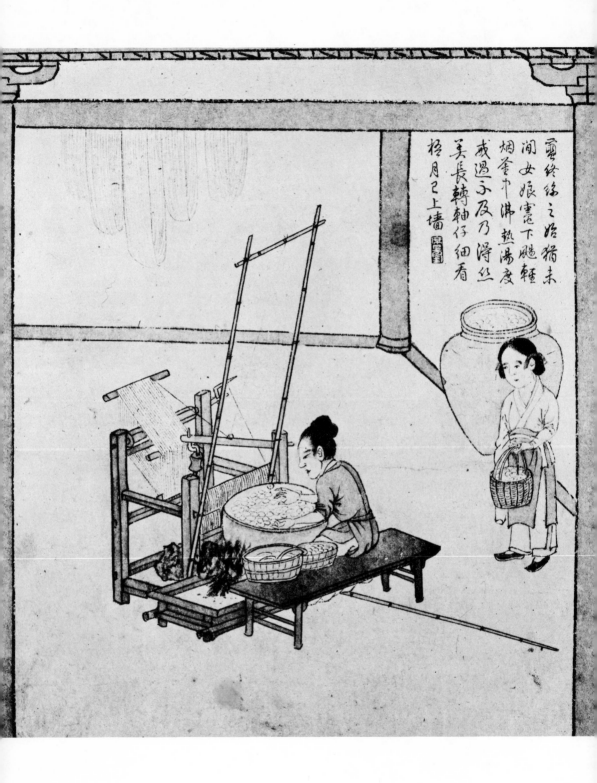

雪繭終絡之始猶未
闌女娘慮下颭輕
烟釜中沸熱湯度
戒過子及乃浮丝
美長轉軸仔細看
格月乙上墙

TRADE ROUTES SERIES
Prepared under the general editorship
of Edward R. Sammis

EAST
TO CATHAY
THE SILK ROAD

by ROBERT COLLINS

McGRAW-HILL BOOK COMPANY
New York · Toronto · London · Sydney

Library of Congress Catalog Card Number: 68-15465
1234567890 HDBP 7543210698

For Jane and Herman
who helped

CONTENTS

The Roman world at the time of the Battle of Carrhae, 53 BC, included most countries that bordered on the Mediterranean.

The Deadly Banners of Carrhae

Like other Romans of his time, the renowned General Marcus Licinius Crassus had never heard of silk. His sole concern one summer day in the year 53 BC was to destroy his foe, the barbarian Parthians (Persians). He had marched from Syria across the Euphrates river and had driven the enemy deep into the billowing sand dunes of what is now Iran. Near the city of Carrhae, his seven legions of men-at-arms and horsemen—some 40,000 in all—had just caught up with the Parthians. As the sun rose they were buckling into their armor.

Roman legions marched into Central Asia.

The Romans, although eager to fight, were not without misgivings. The days past had been full of evil omens. In Syria a few weeks before, Crassus had stumbled and fallen as he left the temple of Hierapolis. He had regained his feet quickly, remarking wryly, "Such is old age! But no weapon, you may be sure, shall fall from my hands!" Although still vigorous at sixty-two, he might be too feeble to provide effective leadership.

Then, crossing the Euphrates, his horse had stumbled, bolted, and drowned. Later still, making a sacrifice to the gods before this battle, Crassus dropped the sheep's entrails in the midst of the ceremony.

This very morning, he had absent-mindedly donned a plain black garment instead of the proud scarlet of a

Romans wore overlapping armor, carried heavy shields. They are shown here making camp (from Trajan's column).

Roman general. He had corrected his error hastily only after someone pointed it out. None of the signs, however, gave warning of the decisive role that silk was to play in his career.

In spite of the portents, Crassus was supremely confident. He had commanded many a winning army in his day and these barbarians had shown no sign of fight.

10

True, they had stopped retreating at last, but this was all to the good. Crassus welcomed the chance to do battle, after which he could go home.

He ranged his troops in a classic Roman battle style called the "testudo" formation: hollow squares with twelve men on each side standing so close together that their shields overlapped like fish scales. Protecting each hollow square of foot soldiers was a prancing squadron of cavalry. Surely no enemy could breach these solid blocks of steel.

But it was the familiar story of an outmoded form of warfare suddenly facing a new, flexible style. The Parthians were mobile and tricky, and, in the manner of guerrillas, they refused to fight on the enemy's terms.

They evidently understood psychological warfare, also. To the Romans they looked more like beasts than men. They wore their hair long and bunched over their foreheads. Shaggy animal skins hung over their shoulders. They began the attack with noise—wild inhuman cries and the thump of hide-covered drums hung with bronze bells and copper rings. The sound, so the historian Plutarch wrote a century and a half later, was a "low dismal tone, a mixture of a wild beast's roar and a harsh thunder peal."

The Romans stood momentarily terrified at the uproar. Then the Parthians threw off their skin cloaks to reveal thick dazzling steel helmets and breastplates. Even their horses were armor-clad. Suddenly they swooped in, unleashing a torrent of long arrows from powerful bows—weapons that made Roman bows look like toys. The arrows literally nailed the hands of the Romans to their shields and their feet to the ground. Sometimes two men were impaled with a single shot.

Persian war wagons had sharp side scythes to mow down the enemy.

Again and again the Parthians swept near, kicking up clouds of dust, wheeling just beyond reach of Roman swords, and releasing a fresh volley of arrows as they galloped away. (So the phrase "Parthian shot" was added to our language, meaning any damaging last-minute blow by word or deed.)

The Roman general's son, Publius, led a charge and died. The Parthians mounted his head on a spear and paraded it before the shattered legions. "This, O my countrymen, is my own peculiar loss!" Crassus cried, "But if anyone be concerned for my love of this best of sons, let him show it in revenge. . . ."

Roman shields blocked enemy arrows.

For a time the Romans doggedly held their ground. Then just at noon when the sun was highest, the Parthians staged their coup. As they charged the Romans with their drums sounding, they unfurled their banners. These were of a gleaming, shimmering material such as Rome had never seen before, brilliant in color, embroidered with gold. Shining like fire, the banners spelled power and invincibility. The Romans—exhausted and suffering from wounds and thirst, their "invincible" testudo shattered—broke ranks in terror before this awesome sight, and fled.

Over the next two days the Parthians had little left to do but murder the wounded and mop up the stragglers. Some 20,000 Romans died and another 10,000 were taken prisoner. Crassus himself was lured into a trap and killed, and his head was sent home to the Parthian king.

It was one of the greatest defeats in Roman history. To the survivors, the side effects went unnoticed at the time: the glittering banners were the Romans' introduction to silk. It was a rude beginning, but silk was soon to be the most coveted item in their world and the basis of one of the greatest trade routes in history.

This road was to stitch the known world together from Pacific to Atlantic, and to mirror that area's history. Cities, empires, and civilizations rose to power and fell to waste along its way. A motley assortment of explorers, adventurers, merchants, warriors, and priests trudged its ruts. Ideas, philosophies, religions, and inventions flowed intermittently back and forth.

Even when wars raged around it and kingdoms toppled, the silk trade usually pressed on. It was more important than empires. Silk was prized beyond belief, at times literally worth its weight in gold. It was a symbol of luxury, a treasure to be haggled for, fought for, died for.

Seventeen years later another small event was recorded, but its significance, too, went unnoticed by historians for centuries. In 36 BC a Chinese force attacked and captured a Central Asian town, Li-chien, some 3,700 miles east of Rome. It had been held by another band of barbarians, the Huns, but in the town the Chinese captured 145 foreign mercenary soldiers. There were three peculiar aspects to this town. The name, Li-chien, was one of the Chinese names later applied to the Roman Empire. It was protected by wooden stockades, a Roman technique. Its soldiers employed the testudo formation of overlapping shields.

Raiding as they went, the Huns terrorized everyone.

Were those nameless soldiers of Li-chien a remnant of Crassus' army? If so, the battle of Carrhae provided another link with the history of silk because these foreign mercenaries were almost certainly the first "westerners" to set foot on the mighty Silk Road.

The Silk Road was not so much a *road* as a *route*.

It was one of several by which silk found its way from China to the West. During the first fifteen centuries of the Christian era, "The West" meant the lands bordering the Mediterranean Sea. Silk traveled by various routes over the centuries, depending on the pressures of the endless wars and the ever-shifting empires of Asia. Some of the silk was transported from the interior of southern China to the coast, thence by sea to India. Some went overland to India, then by sailing vessels through the Indian Ocean and the Red Sea to the market places of the Middle East. But the most important, the most romantic, and the most hazardous route ran overland, due west from Cathay.

Even this road had various forks and alternates, and many of the town or city names of those times have either changed or vanished altogether. Nevertheless one can trace its general course on a map of today. The road began in China's Kansu province at Siam, meandering northwest toward Inner Mongolia between the Nan Shan Mountains and the Gobi Desert. There it forked to either side of the Takla Makan Desert in China's Sinkiang province, which lies between Tibet and Russia, plunging through the Pamir Mountains into the southern tip of Russia. Then it moved through Iran and Iraq (sometimes veering into what is now Afghanistan), spreading out like the fingers on a hand into Turkey, or Syria, or Lebanon, or Israel, or Egypt. Its ultimate destination was Rome.

Such was the main route, although many of the countries just named did not even exist in those times. A dreadfully perilous route it was, too, with dizzying mountain trails to be traversed, bitter cold, fierce summer heat, and blinding sandstorms. Travelers were be-

Caravan camel sculpture

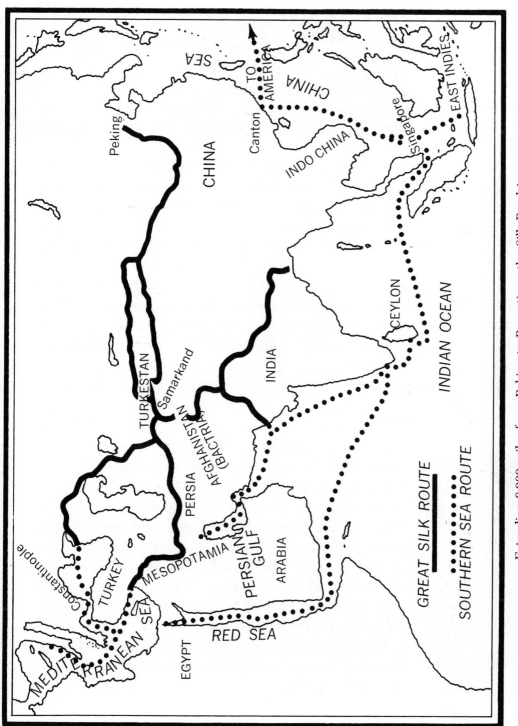

Extending 6,000 miles from Peking to Byzantium, the Silk Road is the longest road in continuous use in history. It goes back to 2500 B.C. Dotted line shows alternate sea route.

GREAT SILK ROUTE
SOUTHERN SEA ROUTE

Silk caravan set out from Peking over mountainous terrain such as this.

set not only by weird ghostly shapes and sounds—spooks and goblins, the caravaners insisted—but also by very real and bloodthirsty bandits—Huns from the North or hillmen from Tibet.

It took ten months to a year traveling time, although no one man normally followed the silk all the way from East to West. Silk passed through many a greedy middleman on a journey which was long, even by our standards. It would have been 4,200 miles as the crow flies, and was actually 6,000 miles with all the twists and turns. This was a quarter-way around the world of today and, in those times, the length of almost the entire *known* world.

Then, and long after, the "world" was a flat constricted area bounded by Gaul, Spain, and the islands of Britain to the west, the Scandinavian countries to the north, the Indian Ocean and northern Africa to the south, and to the east, the mysterious land of the Chinese. In the time of Crassus, few Romans had more than a vague awareness of territory east of Persia. The Chinese, similarly, heard only the faintest rumors of a world west of Central Asia. The two great empires were little oases of civilization, separated by vast, uninhabited stretches and barbarian hordes.

Though he little knew or cared, the ill-fated Crassus in his last hours on earth had glimpsed one of the wonders of the ages.

Hsi-ling-shih and the Royal Worm

The Princess Hsi-ling-shih was a dainty and thoughtful little woman. She had dark almond-shaped eyes, thick black hair piled high in the elaborate headdress favored by privileged Chinese ladies of the twenty-seventh century BC, and the elegant flowing robes befitting the chief concubine of the Emperor Huang-ti. Like all ladies of the court, she also had plenty of time for contemplation.

One day, according to legend, while strolling in the palace gardens, she noticed a small gray worm on a mulberry tree, spinning its cocoon. It was a common sight; China had millions of such worms and trees. But the princess watched a while as the little creature wove the fine glistening threads around itself. Such threads, she remembered, were sometimes used for the strings of musical instruments; wise men said that the Emperor Fu Hsi had first used them in this manner two or three centuries before.

Silkworm spinning cocoon

Such strong shiny threads—she gently touched them. Suddenly Hsi-ling was seized with an idea. If these strands could be unwound for use in musical instruments, could they not also be unraveled and woven into garments? She experimented. The threads were stuck together with a gummy substance and had to be loosened with boiling water. This was only the beginning of the tech-

17

niques which had to be learned. But, at this moment, the silk industry was born. The silkworm of Hsi-ling-shih was a royal worm indeed.

It was eons from the time of the imaginative princess to the years of the Silk Road. At first only Chinese royalty could produce and use silk. It was used in the most exalted places: sunshades for the emperors, for instance, and banners for the temples of the gods. As it became more plentiful it was utilized for clothing—but only for members of the imperial court. The etiquette of silken robes was very specific. Inside the palace the emperor, and only the emperor, wore robes of purest white. Outside, for processions and state functions, a pecking order of colors was laid down. The emperor, his first wife, and the heir to the throne wore yellow, the color of the sun. His other wives wore violet, as did officers of highest rank. Those of second and third rank wore red. The rest stepped out in black.

Around the twelfth century BC the imperial power began to decline and China broke up into many powerful, small states, each with its own prince. The favor of being able to use and wear silk was extended to these princes, whereupon each sought to outdazzle the other. Good taste and simplicity were swamped in a riot of color. Demand for the material increased, and peasants were assigned the task of cultivating the worms. The use of silk became permissible—and naturally popular—with soldiers, landowners, civil servants, and merchants. Around the sixth century BC the great teacher Confucius noted in one of his books that he liked to wear a silken cap *anyway* although it was cheaper and therefore more vulgar than any other textile. By the fifth century BC, at least six Chinese provinces were producing silk.

Sir Aurel Stein discovered this first century BC silk in Chinese Turkestan. (Note horsemen and dragon figures.)

The cause of this revolution, then and for centuries after, the creature that caught Princess Hsi-ling's attention, was and is anything but exotic. The silkworm moth, *bombyx mori*, is ash-white and about one inch long. It lays 500 or more eggs in four to six days, and dies soon after. The eggs are like pinpoints—one hundred of them weigh only one gram. From one ounce of eggs come about 30,000 worms which eat a ton of ripe mulberry leaves and produce twelve pounds of raw silk.

The breeding technique devised by the princess and her successors has changed little in form, although a great deal in technical detail, over the ages. It is precise work demanding the greatest care. The eggs must be kept at 65 degrees F, increasing gradually to 77 degrees, at which point they hatch. The emerging caterpillar is black and about one-twelfth of an inch long, with a spine-like horn at its tail.

Its function in life is simple: to eat, sleep, grow fat, and spin a cocoon. The job of its keeper is far more complex. The temperamental worm must be watched day and night. It must have scrupulously clean, disinfected, well-ventilated quarters kept at 75 to 80 degrees F. Draughts, loud noises, or strong odors such as fish, tobacco, or even sweat will upset its delicate system. Generally worms are kept in trays for easy handling and stacking on shelves.

During its feeding period—some thirty-two days broken by twenty-four-hour sleep intervals on the 6th, 12th, 18th, and 26th days, and four sheddings of skin—the worm consumes twenty times its own weight of mulberry leaves. The leaves must be freshly chopped, dry but not dried-out, and replaced every half hour. During its final waking period the worm gorges itself, growing to a length of three or three-and-a-half inches.

Silkworms are being fed on the right and cocoons are being sorted on the left.

When the time has come to begin spinning, the silkworm lets its watchers know it is ready by raising the forepart of its body and weaving from side to side. It is promptly whisked into spinning trays or frames. They may resemble latticework, or be compartmented, or contain piles of straw or even branches. Whatever their appearance, they always simulate the natural environment of mulberry trees where worms normally would spin their cocoons.

The thread is produced in two tubular glands that run parallel to the intestinal tract. These unite into a single strand which comes out of the worm's jaws. Another secretion, called sericin, sticks the threads together. The worm's contractions force a continuous thread of silk from its body.

The time has come for the silkworm to change into a moth. During the period of metamorphosis, for protection, it spins a cocoon around itself by moving its head constantly in a figure-8 pattern. The spinning process lasts several days.

Before the moth bursts out, an action which would break the threads and make it impossible to unravel a continuous strand, the undeveloped moth, or chrysalis, is suffocated by exposure to steam or to heat in an oven. The cocoons are put into boiling water, which dissolves the bonding material, and the thread is carefully wound on reels. The silk is now ready for weaving and dyeing.

For centuries this procedure was followed in China, a favored area for silk production because worms and mulberry trees were plentiful and painstaking care for detail was inbred in the people. The early Chinese supplemented their craftsmanship with ritual, to please the gods and chase out demons. Every spring, the empress

Natural-sized chrysalis

Moth, eggs, chrysalises

Worm spinning in a frame

Chrysalis grows in cocoon

herself inaugurated the silk-raising season, for silk production was the work of women all over China. During this season the ladies of the court made a sacrifice. They wore no fine clothes or ornaments, indicating that their chief concern was the making of silk.

The peasant women—grandmothers, mothers, daughters—did the real work, of course. Pampering the worm, and weaving and dyeing silk occupied six months of their year. Plain at first, their handiwork grew more and more decorative. By 1000 BC elaborate patterns were being woven into the fabric: dragons, wavelike bands, reproductions of real animals, zig-zag lines, stylized palm leaves, shell-like figures.

Although the use of silk became widespread in China, its value remained high. Eventually even the common people were able to wear garments of silk, though they did not have the elegant embroidery of delicate feathers or gold. Nor did they have on their tea tables the cups of lacquered silk that were customary with the nobility or the very wealthy.

Noble ladies raised silkworms from moth to chrysalis.

Chinese family engaged in silkworm culture behind royal courtyard.

Preparing raw silk was often a family enterprise.

Silk achieved importance in a multitude of other ways. Until the invention of paper, people wrote on it. It became a popular form of currency—a counterpart of paper money. Rewards, bounties, and even taxes were paid in silk. It found its way so thoroughly into the Chinese language that 230 of the 5,000 most common characters of the Mandarin "alphabet" have silk as their "key."

As for the little Princess Hsi-ling, she was venerated and forever after known as "Little House of Silk." Her discovery swept through an empire and soon began to move west over the caravan trails.

Cocoons were dropped in boiling water to kill the chrysalis.

A single strand of silk from each cocoon is spun with others on reels.

How Silk Moved Out into the World

To the highly civilized people of ancient China, their neighbors the Huns, who wandered over the barren steppes of eastern Europe, were barbarians in every sense. These wild, unkempt nomads knew nothing of literature, music, or art. Never pausing to tend the soil and raise a crop, they roamed from pasture to pasture, waterhole to waterhole, carrying their womenfolk and their worldly goods with them, killing and pillaging wherever they went.

When the Huns brought back the head of an enemy they were rewarded with a bowl of wine—which they frequently drank from the enemy's skull. They were allowed to keep all their booty. This practice encouraged them to slaughter and plunder. It was as protection against the Huns that the Chinese constructed that wonder of the world, the Great Wall, which snaked its way 1,500 miles along the northern perimeter of the empire.

By 138 BC Wu-ti, sixth emperor of the Han dynasty, decided to rid himself of this recurring menace. He planned to make an alliance with the Yueh-chih, a people living to the west of the Huns and also harassed periodically by them. The goal was to encircle and eventually crush the barbarians. For his emissary Wu-ti chose Chang Ch'ien, the first of many ambassadors who carried

Shaggy two-hump camels were ideally suited to travel over the Silk Road with its great extremes—desert heat and mountain cold.

China toward the West. Chang Ch'ien took with him bolts of beautiful silk, which he used as a form of barter or bribe. In this way he blazed the trail for the Great Silk Road which was to come later.

Chang, who enjoyed the emperor's confidence as his trusted adviser, was known as a man of great strength and courage. He was in need of both, for he was about to venture into unknown perils. Of only one danger was he sure: he and his pitifully small force of one hundred men would inevitably come in contact with the barbarians.

The mission got off to a bad start. No sooner were Chang Ch'ien and his party in Hun territory (now Kansu province in northwest China) than they were captured. The Huns refrained from slaughtering them, but they did hold them prisoners for ten years. Chang Ch'ien was

Chinese soldiers needed strong horses.

forced to marry a Hun woman, who bore him a son. In time Chang escaped and diligently resumed his assignment.

At last he reached Kokand, 10,000 *li* or roughly 3,300 miles from home. En route he must have traversed one of the worst sections of the later Silk Road, the awesome Gobi and Takla Makan Deserts, but history tells nothing of his miseries.

In Kokand he found towns, farmers, craftsmen, and, most remarkable, strong horses that were a cross between domestic mares and wild mountain stallions. They "sweated blood," and because of this were believed to have mystical qualities. Actually, this phenomenon was caused by parasites that burrowed under the horses' skin around the shoulder and back, causing small swellings that burst and bled.

These animals were a distinct improvement over the little Mongolian steppe horses of Wu-ti's cavalry. Horses were not shod in those days and normally their hooves wore down quickly, making them useless. The "blood-sweating" horses were powerfully built and their tough hooves withstood the wear and tear of rocky trails. Chang longed for some of the Kokand horses, but the ruler of the area refused to sell him any.

The prince, however, did provide guides to the Yueh-chih, but here again Chang failed. The Yueh-chih had no desire to join forces with far-off China and thereby antagonize the neighboring Huns. Chang turned back home. He was recaptured by the Huns, escaped again, and thirteen years after his departure—with only one of his original one hundred men—arrived once more at the emperor's court.

He was richly rewarded, not only for his perseverance,

This tomb tile—a horse and four phoenixes—dates from the third to fifth century BC.

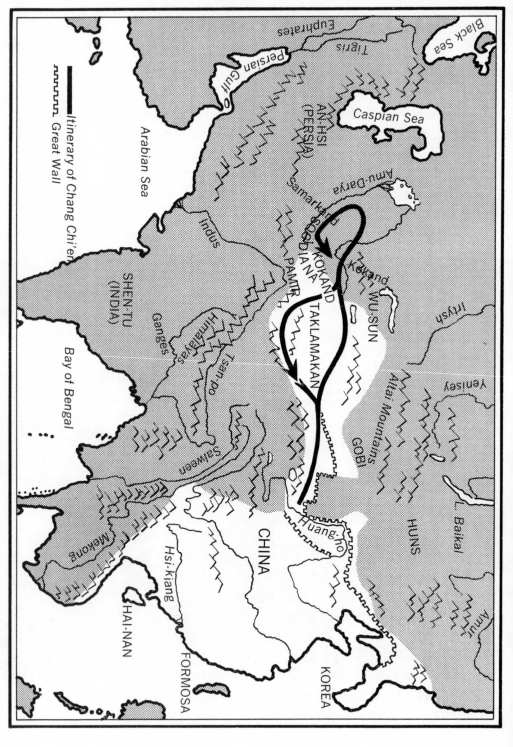

Dotted line shows the westward journey of Chang Chien, a Chinese diplomat, about 100 BC. To win friends on his journey, Chang carried silk.

but for the information he brought concerning far-away
lands.   Now Wu-ti dreamed of extending his empire
into Central Asia.   Year after year he sent embassies
west—as many as ten separate missions within a twelve-
month period, sometimes made up of several hundred
men.   Some of them were gone for as long as ten years.
Always they carried presents, of which silk was the most
common and the most esteemed.

Ladies preparing woven
silk (from eighth-century
scroll)

Wu-ti yearned for Kokand horses almost as much as
he longed for an expanded empire.   The horses, he cal-
culated, would be best suited to carry the legions which
would conquer new territories for him.   But neither silk
nor gold could buy them.   Indeed, the prince of Kokand
had one group of persistent Chinese emissaries murdered
for its efforts to obtain his horses.   Wu-ti sent an army
to avenge them.   It was lost.   In a rage he marshaled
the full resources of his empire.   Peasants labored for
weeks preparing nonperishable food, such as cooked and
dried rice, for the troops; warriors armed themselves
with enormous crossbows.   Finally an expedition of 60,000
men, 30,000 horses, and supply forces with oxen, donkeys,
and camels, marched on Kokand.

Only half the army survived the grueling trip.   The
emperor's men beseiged Kokand for forty days.   In the
end the ruler was forced to hand over thirty blood-
sweating horses, and some thousands of lesser breeds.

It was a rash, costly mission.   Only 10,000 of the original 60,000 men reached home, and only a few horses.
But to Wu-ti the horses were the important thing—human
lives were as expendable as chaff—and from this small
nucleus grew a new breed of Chinese war horse.

Wu-ti and the emperors who followed him did their
best to consolidate these gains.   Their people inched

westward, after finally subduing the Huns. They built forts, set up military posts, filled colonies with some 700,000 people, many of whom were deported criminals and other people that they forced to move. Occupation troops served double duty as farmers. Keeping these colonies protected and obedient was an almost constant problem. But their presence did make possible a permanent road to the West.

In this century prior to the birth of Christ, Central Asia was made up of hundreds of states. Some consisted of only a few families. Some were huge and powerful, such as Parthia (Persia). Chang Ch'ien had heard of Parthia in his wanderings.

The tireless Wu-ti had sent many legations there. The first, dispatched about 105 BC, was met at the eastern frontier by 20,000 Parthian horsemen who, mellowed by many gifts no doubt, hospitably conducted the Chinese to the capital. A Parthian ambassador returned to China with gifts that delighted the emperor: an ostrich egg and some conjurors.

From then on trade relations between China and Persia flourished. At last Chinese silks moved into the outer world. The secret of silk, however, was to remain locked inside China for many more centuries to come. So it was that some fifty years later Parthian silks—already well-known in that country—were to awe Crassus' legions at Carrhae. And so, too, the Chinese began to realize that there were many peoples, other than the troublesome Huns, inhabiting the outer world.

The caravans plodded steadily between Parthia and Serametropolis (now Siam), along what those travelers called the *Imperial Highway*. It was the first leg of what we now know as the Silk Road.

Chinese mandarin wears silk.

On The Road

As he stood at the gates of Serametropolis in the early morning light, the writer Hsuan Tsang was elated and a little frightened. He had waited long for this chance to travel with a silk caravan to the far western lands. But the friend who had come to wish him farewell was solemn.

"You are a fool," he warned. "I have heard much of these caravans. Gone for months. Attacked by bandits. In the Great Desert there is no water and there are storms. And demons—demons that lead a man away from his caravan—far, far away until he dies."

"I know of these things," Hsuan Tsang said. "But it is a great adventure."

"What value are you to this caravan?" his friend scoffed. "You are not a merchant of silk. You cannot drive a camel."

"The head man has welcomed me." Hsuan Tsang smiled wryly. "He said any man who can bear a sword or bend a bow is of use to him. Wish me a safe journey. The animals are ready now. I will see you again, one day."

His friend nodded, smiled, and turned back into the city. The caravan was a noisy bedlam with the bellowing of camels, the barking of dogs, the cries of drivers. The last of the kneeling beasts was loaded. Great bales

Chinese ink was made in cakes—some decorated, as above.

and droopy rolls of silk were fastened to saddles which were padded and fattened with fodder.

Hsuan Tsang strolled nearer to watch. The shaggy Bactrian camels were remarkable; the best possible creatures to have for companions in the months ahead. They were about seven feet high, with two humps and three-toed feet that found support in sand. They could travel two or three miles per hour bearing a 400-pound load. They were able to live on the sparsest and coarsest of plants—thorns, twigs, leaves, dried grass—and to store fat in their humps which they would later draw on for food. They could also turn the stored fat into water.

The caravan drivers said they could travel as long as seventeen days without water. When they reached a water hole, they would stock up again with as much as twenty-five gallons in ten minutes. Hsuan Tsang noticed the double row of protective lashes on their eyes, the hair-covered ear openings, the nostrils which could close tight in a sandstorm. Admirable beasts! They will probably stand the journey far better than I, Hsuan thought as he checked his long cloak, skin boots, and the head covering that could be drawn around his face.

With a cry from the headman, the caravan was on its feet and moving off, single file, in the early sunshine, with perhaps one hundred animals and as many men. There was safety in numbers on the caravan trail.

Bells tinkled from the camels' necks; feet thudded softly on the red clay soil. All day the long line of travelers plodded through the flat landscape, covering a distance of some sixty *li* (about twenty miles) before the leader shouted for a halt. Some rice and a bit of meat, sleep under the stars, then on again the next day. In eighteen days they reached the city of Lanchow.

Hsuan Tsang rode with a caravan into the desert.

Here they paused to rest and to take on fresh provisions. Once more they headed out through the undulating countryside to the northwest. Suddenly on the right Hsuan Tsang glimpsed a yellow-gray snakelike structure winding up hill and down valley, extending for miles off into the distance.

"The Great Wall," said a camel driver. So, at last. This was the Great Wall which held back the Huns from his country! Hsuan Tsang studied it with awe. It was artfully built from local materials: large clay bricks alternated with bundles of tamarisk branches. Along its length at intervals were watchtowers and soldiers on guard.

That night the caravan paused in the lee of a watchtower and Hsuan Tsang visited the garrison. It was a snug little bastion: a fireplace, sleeping platforms of stamped clay, a narrow entrance with two stout posts holding a heavy door and bars. The handful of soldiers in their black linen tunics were friendly.

"It is always good to see the caravans," said one. "What news from the cities?"

Hsuan Tsang told all he knew and asked in return, "What is the life like here?"

Camels, horses, mules, and travelers of all kinds made up a Silk Road caravan.

The soldier shrugged. "The days go slowly. There are horses to tend, water to fetch, weapons to care for." He nodded toward a sword, a shield, a crossbow, and 150 arrows. "Each of us has these. We play with dice at night. But always there is a lookout and always that." He pointed to a heap of timber, laid ready for a bonfire.

"What is that for?"

"If the Hun comes, we signal. Flame by night, smoke by day. For many Huns, much smoke, much flame. So the signal goes, along the Wall." The soldier shivered. "I do not like this place. The Huns come out of nowhere. They cut a man to pieces, little by little, while he still lives!"

Hsuan Tsang shuddered too, and slept close by the fires that night. The caravan trudged on, day after day, week after week. On the left the Nan Shan Mountains loomed. On the right the Great Wall fell away and disappeared. But still, here and there, stood a watchtower with a garrison. The brilliant Chinese General Pan Ch'ao had seized this land for the empire and with his armies repeatedly roamed it and gave it as much protection as he could.

Now the caravan approached Yumen. On the right the Gobi Desert raised its ocean of sand dunes. The heat was intense but there was no opportunity for stopping by day, unless the headman decreed a halt. This was the law of the trail. A delay of hours might stretch into days, which might mean not enough water in the skin waterbags to reach the next oasis. A man or beast who fell behind could expect no help. Hsuan Tsang noticed, uncomfortably, that the trail, normally spotted with camel droppings, was often marked now with skeletons—animal and human.

The Silk Road, for much of its length,
ran parallel to the Great Wall of
China.

A pause at Yumen for eating and drinking, tending
the raw backs of the camels, cleaning weapons, patching
boots.   Then on toward the clay-walled city of Tuhn-
wang—and a decision.

"Will it be the north trail around the Takla Makan
or the south?" the drivers asked the caravan leader one
night.   He thought in silence.

"The north way takes one through Hami, Kara
Shahr, Kucha, and Aksu," a driver said to Hsuan.   "Ah,
Aksu.   Do you know Aksu?   It means white water, they
say.   The water pours down from the mountains cold,
clean.   And there are fields and melons, and plums and
grapes.   I hope we go the north way."

"The north way is closer to the Huns," the headman
said.   "I learned of them in Yumen.   The Huns are riding out often, these nights.   I think we shall take the
south way."

"The storms are very bad to the south of Takla Makan," an older driver said.

"I choose the storms over the Huns," the caravan
leader said, and that was the end of the discussion.
They moved out the next morning, and now Hsuan Tsang
could see the Takla Makan Desert—first just a yellow-
orange line on the horizon, moving, shifting.   Then, as
they drew nearer, the drifting dunes of sand curved
away.   Here and there, sharp barren salt flats cut at the
camels' feet.   No water could be found, and soon even
thorny vegetation disappeared.

Day after day they plodded through oceans of yellow
sand, mirages' glittering over the wastes, sun breathing
fire on their backs.   (Had Hsuan Tsang known, the heat
at its worst reached 150 degrees F.)   Once in a while

they stopped and dug a well in the sand and brackish water seeped into it. Sometimes, miracle of miracles, a clear spring welled up from some underground channel. But for the most part they sipped water sparingly from the skin bags. The camels went without; only a little to moisten their lips on the worst days. As the heat increased, the caravan leader ordered that they travel at night, and navigate by the stars.

"Stay close," he warned, "and listen for the bells."

They reached the oasis of Lop Nor, the first of several on the desert fringe fed by streams from the mountains to the south. What a joy to see green grass and fresh water. Then on again. A sandstorm struck. It began with a slowly rising wind and a thickening yellow-red haze. The sand began to dance in clouds and columns, a devilish dance, swallowing up all things on the ground for a dozen feet or more without blotting out the fierce sun. Soon it was impossible to see anything but the man and camel directly ahead.

The men of the caravan stopped early, setting markers in the sand so that they could find their direction in the morning. The wind increased, driving sand and salt into mouths, noses, ears, eyes, clothing, packs, everything. It grew into a high-pitched moan.

"The voices . . . I hear the voices!" an old driver shrieked.

Detail from dragon scroll

The caravan leader cursed him. "Be quiet, you fool, it is only the wind and the sand. You will frighten my men."

The old man huddled down but spoke again, loud enough for Hsuan Tsang and those nearest to hear him.

"Say what you will," he moaned, "I know them. They are out there, the goblins, the demons! They sing, they wail, they beat on drums! I have heard them before."

"It is true," another driver whispered. "Once on a caravan another man and I strayed and were lost. Suddenly we heard the tramp of many feet. 'It is our caravan,' cried the one with me, and he ran toward it and disappeared. But it was *not* our caravan. It was *them*. I never saw him again!"

The old man whimpered again. "Sometimes they call a man's name. I have known them to call a man's name and he goes to answer and he is lost in the storm. Sometimes they lead a man away with lights. Ah, if the gods will only let me live this night, I will never follow a caravan again!"

The men passed a sleepless night. The storm raged a second day, and a third. The caravan moved only a few *li* each day. At night, the ghostly noises returned. Was it really the wind? Hsuan Tsang was an intelligent man. He did not believe in demons, and yet. . . . The storm ended on the fourth day and the caravan, missing three camels and one man, struggled on to Charchan; then to Khotan; then another 770 *li* to Yarkand. They had spent nearly two months in the terrible desert.

Yarkand, at last! Here the trail led into the oasis and straight into a noisy shouting bazaar like a tunnel. Peddlers tugged at Hsuan Tsang's sleeve to tempt him

An artist gives his conception of demons, goblins, and evil spirits believed to inhabit the wilder stretches of the old road.

with skins and food and trinkets. There was time for rest again and then on to the great Stone Tower, a landmark on the Silk Road, where caravans often congregated. Here the leader learned that a few miles north, in the terminal city of Kashgar, he could sell his cargo to another caravan from the West.

There on an open field one day, Hsuan Tsang watched a curious scene. The traders from his land—Sericans as the others called them—faced these men from the place called Parthia to the west. The bales of silk were placed between them. Hands were buried in the voluminous robes. Only the fingers showed, and so the bargaining began, by sign language. The silk changed hands; the Chinese traders accepted gold and glorious beads and baubles of glass that came from a far-off land beyond Parthia. Of the goods they had to sell the less said the better, so far as they were concerned. They wanted not a word of their silk-growing process to slip out.

"Are there none here that speak their language?" Hsuan Tsang asked. At last a man of Kashgar stepped forward and for a price agreed to act as interpreter.

"Where do you go from here?" he asked one of the traders.

The man of Parthia pointed to the Pamirs.

"What is it like?"

"High. Dangerous. The trails are very narrow, the width of a packhorse only, with high rock on one side and, on the other, nothing. Sometimes there are flatlands with grasses and blue and white flowers and that is good. But there is snow, as well, that comes quickly and blocks the passes."

"You travel with horses?"

"Or yaks. Or mules. A few always fall. Sometimes a man falls, too. There are swift rivers to cross. One lays logs across them and hopes that the footing is safe. A sudden, heavy rain can cause the rivers to rise quickly. If the caravan is in a narrow pass between high rocks the floods come and sweep everything away. Many die."

"A very hard trip, then?"

"It is difficult to breathe in high places. The snow hurts the eyes, the cold hurts the ears, and there are many sicknesses. Yes, it is a very hard trip."

"And beyond," Hsuan Tsang asked eagerly. "What countries are beyond?"

"I do not know. We pass through the Pamirs to Samarkand, a great city of riches and spices. Others go from there. I have heard the names of Merv and Shahrud, Hamadan and Palmyra and Antioch. And far beyond that, they say, past a sea, is the land from which these beads come."

The Parthian turned back to his caravan. Hsuan Tsang turned to his and made ready for the journey home. Behind him the silk moved slowly on toward the rich and idle people of Rome, who knew and cared nothing of the distances and bartering, the suffering and death lying behind this shiny prize that came to them along the road from Cathay.

The Soft and
Silken Days of Rome

While silk made its slow, painful way toward the West, the Romans of the early Christian era knew little of the place where it originated. No Roman soldiers had set foot beyond Parthia, which they often fought but never conquered. As silk found its way into Rome, the people came up with the name "sericum" (seric cloth), apparently derived secondhand from the Chinese "ser" (silk). Since the cloth was seric, reasoned the Romans, the people who made it must be Seres. Such was their name for the inhabitants of the land at the other end of the Silk Road, and the extent of their knowledge of it.

They knew even less about how silk was produced. During the reign of Augustus (27 BC–AD 14), the poet Virgil referred to fine fleece which the Seres took with combs from the leaves of trees. Around AD 70–80 Pliny continued the fiction; he wrote of "the Seres who are famous for the wool of their forests. They remove the down from leaves with the help of water and then the women have the double task of unraveling and weaving. It is thanks to these complicated operations in far-off lands that the Roman matron is able to appear in public in transparent garments."

But the source of silk mattered little to the average well-to-do Roman. It was soft, warm, and caressing to

Emperor Augustus

the skin; it had a lustrous sheen, and took dyes handsomely—that was all that was important. It was a luxury item in an age that doted on luxury.

The unification of the Mediterranean by Rome had given industry an unprecedented boost. Things were going well on the battlefields, too. An enormously wealthy ruling class sprang up: governors, generals, landowners, and others who had cashed in on the fruits of war, exploitation, and commerce. They gorged themselves on exotic foods: snails cooked in wine, *foie gras*, oysters from Spain, cockscomb stew. They guzzled wine: at one feast given by the retired general and renowned glutton Lucullus, the guests downed three million liters (well over five million pints).

Young noblemen bathed several times a day and adorned themselves with gold and pearls. Ladies of the court powdered their hair with gold dust and scattered rare plants through their quarters to enjoy briefly their

Wealthy Romans wore togas made of silk.

exotic perfume. Rome was ripe for silk.

Barely fifty years after that first glimpse at Carrhae, silk had caught Rome's fancy. An edict of AD 14 forbade Roman men to wear it because "silk degrades a man." Actually the women were causing more uproar than men, and it all had to do with Pliny's reference to "transparent garments."

Silk in its natural state clung to the female form in a way that was infinitely more pleasing to the eye than Parthian banners. But Roman ladies did not stop at that. For one thing, there was not enough pure silk to go around at first. And, anyway, it was not sexy enough for those freewheeling days. So, they unraveled the close-woven Chinese fabric and rewove it into a flimsy gauze which left little to the imagination. So unlike

Chinese silk was this Roman adaptation that the Chinese, when they eventually saw it, named it "ling," assuming that Rome was growing a special product of its own.

For the average Roman girl-watcher those were golden years, but the moralists raised a fearful outcry. "I see clothes of silk, if clothes they can be called," wrote the philosopher Seneca (4 BC–AD 64), "affording protection neither to the body nor to the modesty of the wearer, and which are purchased for enormous sums from un-

Roman terra cotta shows clinging dress styles.

known people." Pliny told of garments that "render women naked." Other writers waggishly referred to clothes "made of glass."

Roman men—for a while after the ban, at least—had to be content with bedecking themselves with braid or trimmings, called "clavi." These were ornamental bits of dyed or embroidered silk sewn on togas or tunics. The round or oval clavus, generally purple, was really a badge varying in size or shape according to the rank. A wealthy man might add other frills—perhaps squares or parallel stripes.

Soon silk crept back full-scale into male clothing. By AD 218 the teenage Heliogabalus held the all-time record for using up silk. He ruled Rome for four years, until AD 222, and he wore nothing *but* silk: toga, tunic, outer garments, and undergarments. He changed often, as befitted a royal person, *and he never wore the same garment twice.* How much silk he went through in a lifetime or what he did with the discards no one can guess. Heliogabalus, who was Syrian by birth, was no typical Roman. His effeminate behavior so outraged the people that he was forced to step down and was later killed by mutinous palace guards.

But his choice of dress was a fair reflection of the silk orgy that swept through the Roman Empire. By AD 380 Marcellinus Ammianus was able to report, "The use of silk which was once confined to the nobility has now spread to all classes without distinction, even to the lowest."

Nevertheless, the nobility maintained certain luxury items. For instance, emperors gave as favors garments with silken borders into which the emperor's picture was woven.

Emperor Constantine

Emperor Heliogabalus ruled
Rome for four years and
wore nothing but silk.

But right at this time when Rome craved silk most,
the Silk Road caravans were bedeviled by wars, raiders,
and tumbling empires. The tiny world of the third century was in turmoil. The Roman Empire declined. Its
monetary system collapsed. Too much had been lav-
ished on wars, armies, and luxuries. In a typical year,
one historian reported, the goods of foreign lands, which
included much silk from Seres, drained at least fifty million sesterces from Rome. This was equal to about
10,000 pounds of gold. "So dearly do we pay for our
luxuries and our women."

Mines and fields lay abandoned. Civil strife flared.
Foreign trade fell off. The empire's focal point shifted
from Rome to the eastern Mediterranean cities of Antioch, Alexandria, Byzantium. Byzantium was renamed
Constantinople by the Emperor Constantine, and was
made the capital instead of Rome.

At the other end of the Silk Road the Han dynasty
fell apart after four centuries of artistic accomplishment
and territorial gains. Between these two failing empires
the Persians were aggressively expanding, and all along

47

the northern borders barbarians pressed in on civilized nations. For a century and a half the Silk Road traffic, caught in the squeeze, was thin indeed.

Yet the silk came through, often by sea from India. This too was a hazardous route. Sea captains of those days tended to follow the landmarks of the coast, which seemed a surer way of reaching a destination than sailing far out, depending on the stars and the errant winds. But coastal mariners were easy prey for thousands of savage pirates who lurked in the bays, darted out in their flat-bottomed boats, massacred the crews (or, as often, took them prisoner for the slave trade), and carried off their cargoes. Roman warships under Pompey tried to wipe out piracy with only partial success.

Then a Roman sea captain discovered how to use monsoons, the prevailing winds of the Indian Ocean. One day

In Persia, houses like this (both outside and inside shown)

he cast off with the wind, took a more or less direct route
across the ocean, and landed on the west coast of India.
It was more luck than good management, but other sailors
soon perfected the technique. By studying the seasons
they arranged to sail in July with the west-to-east mon-
soon, arriving in late autumn at one of the Indian ports
of Barbaricon, Baryzaga, or Muziris. The reverse mon-
soon brought them home early in the following year. A
one-way voyage, including the trip through the Red Sea,
took about sixteen weeks.

This only partly alleviated Rome's supply problem.
Much of the time Persia controlled the Indian Ocean
as it did the overland route from China. As dominant
middlemen the Persians charged exorbitant prices. It
is virtually impossible to translate them into today's
terms. But in AD 301 the charge for one pound of Chi-

were used in cultivating the silk worm.

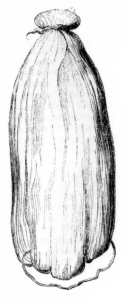

A hank of Persian silk

nese raw silk was very approximately equivalent to $65; for the best purple silk, $800.

By the sixth century, under the Emperor Justinian, a pound of purple silk cost about $1,100. This wild increase was partly due to the disastrous state monopolies of the time. The Byzantines were in an economic trap. They wanted silk. It was like today's automobile—both luxury and necessity. Even the Christian Church was using it liberally for vestments and decorations.

But the government had to maintain some 400,000 soldiers against Persia and the treasury was perpetually empty. So the rulers applied stiff taxes and monopolies. One such move was to control silk from the time it entered the empire in raw bales until the finished garments were sold. Although the state profited from this, the private weavers and dyers, mostly in Syria and Egypt, were reduced to beggary. Some fled to Persia where their craftsmanship was welcomed.

Around the middle of the fourth century the *gynaecea*, or women's textile workshops, were set up under state administration. The emperor's treasurer bought raw material at a ridiculously low price and sold finished products at an equally ludicrous high price, with profit to the state and, usually, himself. In the *gynaecea* silk was dyed and woven under strict supervision. Workers who tried to escape or people who attempted to lure these craftswomen away were harshly punished. And not one fragment of unauthorized silk slipped out.

Expensive dyes boosted the cost. Purple was the coveted color—originally granted only to emperors and later to others of high rank. It ranged through many shades of blue and violet but red-purple was the favorite, symbolically linked with sun, blood, and fire. At times the emperor had his own private shade of purple which no other man dared wear.

The dye came from the glands of a Mediterranean shellfish, the *murex branduris*. Yellow in its original state, it quickly turned red, blue-violet, red-violet, and almost black, in turn, depending on its length of exposure to the sun. The liquid had to be collected in the fall and winter, used immediately, and boiled down to about one-sixteenth of its original volume. Thus a purple toga of ordinary material cost about 10,000 denari (equal to approximately one-fifth of a pound of gold). A toga of purple silk was literally worth its weight in gold, at a time when gold was much more valuable than it is today.

Murex brandaris

So the costs were staggering. The moralists still harped at the wearers of silk. A fifth century bishop denounced people who wore silken garments "like painted walls." If they had to have pictures on their clothes, he sniffed, they should portray Christian subjects instead of animals, landscapes, and scenes from the arena. But none of this deterred the Byzantines. They wanted silk and they were tired of paying exorbitant prices for it, while rulers and foreign middlemen profited. Even the harassed Emperor Justinian longed for a home-grown product. Yet, incredibly, the people of Rome and Byzantium still had no idea of how silk was produced.

The geographer Pausanias, in the second century, came closest to the truth. "The threads which the Seres use for their clothe do not come from the bark of a tree," he wrote. "In their country they have a little animal which the Greeks call *ser* but which they themselves call by quite a different name. In its size this animal is twice as large as the largest beetle. For the rest it resembles the spiders which spin their webs beneath

Silk was painted by hand.

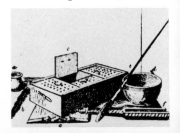

Masterpieces of decorative design
were woven from silks of many colors.

the trees, and like them it has eight legs. The Seres
raise these creatures in special buildings protected from
the heat and cold. The little animals produce very fine
threads which they roll about their feet.

"The Seres feed them for the first four years of their
existence on millet grass but in the fifth year—knowing
that their charges will not live much longer—they give
them a certain kind of green reed. This is the best
possible food for these animals. They eat voraciously
of the reed until they die. It is inside the dead body
that the majority of the thread is found."

Apparently no one heeded Pausanias. Two centuries
later Marcellinus Ammianus wrote, "In the land of the
Seres there are many gloomy forests. The trees are constantly sprinkled with water, as is done with skins that
have to be softened, and from the down so obtained they
weave the fine and delicate material known as Seric
cloth."

It was the myth of Virgil and Pliny all over again.
The merchants of the Silk Road had not, of course, done
anything to correct the fiction. The more mysterious
silk was, they reasoned, the higher its value. But soon
the secret was to be spread throughout the world.

52

A Secret for
All the World

In the year AD 440, so the legend goes, a prince of Khotan—the Silk Road oasis principality on the rim of Takla
Makan, which for centuries had lived on the caravan
trade—courted and won a Chinese princess.

Wedding preparations began. Then the prince dropped
what may have been a well-calculated bombshell into
the arrangements.

"You must understand," he said, "there are no silkworms in my land. You know the law—none can be brought
from your country. It matters not to me, but if you would
raise silk and clothe yourself in it, as is your custom, we
must find a way to bring the silkworms here—unless you
would have me bargain with the caravans, like any
common merchant!"

The princess was confronted with a dreadful dilemma.
She loved her man and her silken garments. But she
also loved her life. Disclosure of the methods of silk
production was punishable by death as was removal
of silkworms or eggs from the country. Thus China had
kept its precious secret for centuries.

The princess and her retinue rode out for Khotan. As
she paused at the frontier, Chinese guards searched the
men and animals of her caravan, but none dared lay a
hand on the princess herself. Had they done so, they

would have found in her voluminous hairpiece a small paper packet of silkworm eggs. Thus, sericulture found its way to Khotan.

This was scant solace to the silk-hungry people of the West, for Khotan kept the secret, too. Why share it with the westerners and kill a good market? So the Byzantine Empire still clamored for silk and the Persians still controlled the traffic, increasing the price of raw silk when it pleased them.

Justinian spread the taste for silk.

Then, around AD 550, two Nestorian monks (an offshoot of the Christian faith) appeared at Emperor Justinian's court.

"We have lived for many years in the country Serinda," the monks announced. "There we have learned the art of raising silk." They could bring this art to Byzantium, the monks continued, with crafty glances at the emperor. Justinian could hardly believe his luck. Hastily he promised them a reward. Off went the monks, prudently taking a detour around Persia. Two years later they were back, bringing with them silkworm eggs—probably stolen from Khotan—in their hollow bamboo staves. Under their supervision the eggs hatched into worms, and the worms spun cocoons. Byzantium was in the silk business at last.

As might have been expected in that ill-fated empire, the emperor bungled a great opportunity. The Mediterranean climate is kind to mulberry trees and silkworms. Byzantium could have quickly raised its own silk and wiped out the greedy Persian middleman. But Justinian ruled that production of cocoons should be an imperial monopoly. The state-operated industry floundered, and the empire still had to look elsewhere for its raw silk.

Monks brought silkworm to Roman emperor in hollow staves.

A fifty-year truce with Persia relieved the emergency for a while.

By now the Romans had spread the taste for silk throughout the western world. In Persia the royal court surrounded itself with silk. The king wore it under his armor; officers, boatmen, and elephant drivers wore it; bed coverings, carpets, and draperies glistened with it.

In Egypt, one caliph hoarded 50,000 lengths of silk damask in his treasury. Another had a tent, made up of sixty-four pieces of silk, worth about $150,000 and laboriously put together by 150 men working for nine years. A new empire of Turks had sprung up in Central Asia. Here, the officers of the guard sitting in two long rows before the khan were all clad in silk.

Silk tunics, along with gold, were used to bribe invading barbarians.

Silk was even beginning to have a civilizing effect on the barbarians. As far back as AD 408 when Alaric, a Goth, beseiged Rome, his price for sparing the city included 5,000 pounds of gold, 3,000 pounds of pepper, 30,000 pounds of silver—and 4,000 tunics of silk. Later in that century, during negotiations between Byzantium and Attila the Hun, the former presented the latter with gifts of silk. In fact, when the emperors discovered the barbarians' childlike delight in "civilized" luxuries, they turned it into a psychological tool.

A barbarian chieftain visiting the emperor in Constantinople, reports a writer of the time, was apt to get this treatment: "Through a dazzling maze of marble corridors, through chambers rich with mosaic and cloth of gold, through long lines of palace guards in white uniforms, amidst patricians, bishops, generals, and senators, to the music of organs and church choirs, he passes, supported by eunuchs, until at last, oppressed with interminable splendor, he falls prostrate in the presence of the silent motionless dramatic figure of the Lord of New Rome, the heir of Constantine, seated on the throne of the Caesars. Before he can rise, the emperor and throne have been caught aloft and, with vestments changed since last he gazed, the sovereign looks down upon him, surely as a god regarding mortal men!" It was enough to make any barbarian go comb his hair and look about him for a silken robe.

In the seventh century the Moslems swamped central Europe. Like the barbarians, they too began by despising the sleek clothing of the decadent people they had conquered. But soon silk worked its spell on them. If one accepts the tales of the *Thousand and One Nights,* silk was everywhere—A vizier's son wears a silk muslin shirt embroidered with gold, trousers of blue silk with a gold tasseled sash, and a silk turban laced with gold and silver. Ladies move in public behind vast veils of blue silk. Shops of silk merchants line the streets of leading cities. . . .

In all lands where silk was prized, the finest fabrics were reserved exclusively for the ruling class. Thus, no matter how widespread its use among the masses, silk never lost its luxury status with the privileged few.

The possession of the secret by the West did not put an end to the Silk Road or the silk trade. On the contrary, Chinese silk remained superior in quality and sometimes exceeded the quantity available elsewhere for centuries. As recently as the nineteenth century, a European report on Chinese sericulture noted ". . . the undeniable superiority of Chinese methods over European ones: they lose scarcely one silkworm in one hundred whereas with us the mortality rate is well over 50 percent."

Silk design of Byzantine emperor

Silk is shipped by boat from silk farm.

Silk was far from the only Chinese export to travel over the Silk Road. Iron and furs—leopard, marten, sable—found their way west. So did some of China's ingenious inventions. One was gunpowder. Another was paper, which the Chinese made as early as the first century AD from silk waste and water, hemp rags, and the pulp found under the bark of the mulberry tree.

For centuries, on the other hand, little of the western world penetrated eastward to China. The Chinese were fond of Roman glass: colored necklaces, cut glass, vessels of all kinds, even though these were much less valuable than silk, jade, or other Oriental treasures. Passing through the hands of many middlemen, such objects eventually reached them. But until about AD 1200 the East-West exchange of goods included little exchange of culture.

Silk culture remained unchanged for centuries.

Jade representation of silk
culture, a desk ornament

For one thing, silk was generally relayed through middlemen such as the Persians or, later, the Turks—and there was a language barrier. A Florentine scholar and diplomat, Brunetto Latini, describes a typical relay point in the silk trade: "Our traders pass over one of their rivers where, on its furthest shores, they find all manner of merchandise. Without speaking, they examine the merchandise and decide by looking at it the price of each piece. And when they have seen it they take away what they wish, leaving in the place of each article its equivalent value. In this wise the natives sell their wares, neither do they desire little or much of ours."

So the Silk Road, through all its centuries, did not become a significant route for exchange of ideas and knowledge until, paradoxically, it was overrun by a people with the most savage reputation of all time. They were nomads from Central Asia, of the same stock as the Turks, but best remembered as the Tartars—the terrible Khans.

The Murderous Khan
Who Worshipped God

As nearly as history can tell us, traffic over the Silk Road persisted and even flourished throughout the reign of Jenghiz Khan and his successors. This seems incredible for the Road lay in the very heart of the Tartar empire which extended from the Pacific to the Black Sea. Wars raged and warriors roamed around the caravans, but still the silk went through—albeit with occasional "protection money" changing hands between traders and warriors.

To realize how the Silk Road survived in those fearsome times, one must understand that strange mixture of savagery and justice, Jenghiz Khan. He was born in the 1160s, in a bleak corner of the northern Gobi Desert. His name was Temuchin. His title—Jenghiz (sometimes Genghis) Khan, the Greatest of Rulers, the Emperor of All Men—came in manhood, around 1206, when he was at the height of his power.

In the palm of his hand, so the legend goes, was a birthmark: a clot of blood. "He will be a great warrior," whispered the people of the tribe. "He will kill many enemies." The boy lived up to the prophecy. In later life, he was known and feared throughout the world. In the next 60-odd years this nomad, son of a herdsman king, would outwit three mighty empires, obliterate

Ugedei, Jenghiz Khan's third son

entire cities, massacre millions, and rule the world from Korea to Hungary, and from China to Iran.

Jenghiz was raised in a fierce age, among the most savage of people, under the toughest conditions. His birthplace was a circular tent of felt, called a *yurt*, with a hole in the top to let light in and smoke out. It was thoroughly portable: when the tribe moved the yurt moved with them, folded into an oxcart.

Like all babies of his time he was raised on mother's and mare's milk, then quickly weaned to whatever food the tribe could find: dogs, wolves, antelope, sheep, foxes, horses, even rats. Every scrap was devoured, even the marrow from bones.

The living habits would have horrified modern mothers. Each Tartar carried a wooden eating bowl that was licked clean after the meal, rinsed with juice from the main cooking pot and emptied back into that pot. Milk pails were never washed—this was bad luck—so a thick crust of hardened milk, mixed with hair and dung, formed on the inside.

Having survived babyhood, young Jenghiz had already proved he was hardy. He next served a Tartar child's apprenticeship, beginning by being accorded the place farthest from the tent fire. In the summer he went on the hunt. In the winter the strongest men ate first, while women, old people, and children battled with the dogs for leftover bones and scraps. He killed his first man at thirteen. Only the strong and vicious survived, and Jenghiz learned his lesson well. He was formulating the philosophy that he proudly expressed in later years: "A man's greatest joy in life is to break his enemies and to take from them all the things that have been theirs and to hold in his arms the most desirable of their

Framework of Tartar yurt

Villages sprang up overnight wherever Tartars wandered.

women." His own father had set that example: Jenghiz's
mother had been on the way to her wedding when his
father snatched her for himself.

As a teenager the boy spotted the first and, according
to history, the truest love of his life: Bortai, the pretty
nine-year-old daughter of another warrior. He asked
for her. His father and Bortai's discussed it, agreed,
and completed the sale. But Jenghiz was not to make
her his wife for seven more years.

A few days later Jenghiz's father was poisoned and
the boy himself was fleeing from enemies. He was caught,
was put into a wooden yoke, escaped, and fought for
his life. He not only lived but rose through innumerable
battles to become Khan of the united Mongol and Tartar peoples. He believed that he had been called by
Heaven to conquer the world.

Sixteenth century idea of
Khan's dress

A tall powerful man with strong features, catlike eyes, wide forehead, and a long beard, he was utterly ruthless in battle. In 1211 he led 250,000 warriors against China. They smashed through the Great Wall with little difficulty, but had to spend five years conquering the nation. In that time they wiped out ninety cities, slaughtered the inhabitants, and sometimes leveled the ruins until not a trace remained.

His Mongol warriors were swift, mobile, and merciless. They rode tough, tireless ponies and were armed with bow, cutlass, and dagger. Their enemies were sometimes nailed to wooden horses, boiled in huge pots, or skinned alive.

From China, Jenghiz turned to Turkestan. First he sent out ambassadors, who were murdered by an imprudent frontier commander; next he sent an army of 700,000. He plundered and burned Bokhara. Then he turned to Samarkand, the great Silk Road center of trade. It was enclosed by walls and fortifications two and a half miles in circumference and guarded by 110,000 men. He captured it.

Samarkand, as did most cities, supplied him with a rich assortment of human trophies. He singled out 30,000 artisans to serve as slaves for his sons and generals. A number of able-bodied men were drafted into military service or general labor. All the pretty girls were reserved for the pleasure of the Khan himself. The rest of the inhabitants were beheaded. Even those who escaped were not necessarily free. One such group was generously granted permission to don Mongolian uniforms and join the Khan's army. When they trudged unsuspectingly into his camp he murdered them.

"The conquered never become their conquerors'

Posterity's idea of Jenghiz Khan, as portrayed in the Russian theater. Although ruthless, he was tolerant of all religions.

friends," Jenghiz warned his followers. "The destruction of the conquered is the conquerors' best guarantee of safety."

In the course of his victories Jenghiz collected some 500 wives and concubines, beauties from all over Asia and Europe. He had a unique grading system. Each captain in his army turned over the most beautiful girls from a defeated city to the colonel. The colonel weeded out the best in *his* opinion, and handed them to the general. *He* culled them again and passed them to the army commander. The commander selected the cream of the crop for Jenghiz Khan.

Jenghiz Khan chose beautiful girls to be his wives and concubines.

Savage as the man was, there were contradictory traces of wisdom and piety in him. He had never learned to write; yet he laid down a code of laws and an efficient system of administration that governed many nations. Oddest of all—ruthless as he was—he permitted religious tolerance. The first of his laws, called the Yassa, was not unlike the first of the Ten Commandments: "It is ordered to believe that there is only one God, creator of Heaven and earth, who alone gives life and death, riches and poverty as it pleases Him, and who has over everything else an absolute power."

Under this law, Nestorians, Buddhists, and Moslems

Tartars, under the leadership of Jenghiz Khan, were savage warriors.

TARTARISCHE MANNEN.
Viri Tartarici.

worshiped unmolested. Travelers, too, could cross his
kingdom unharmed. Pillage and kill though they might
in wartime, the people of Jenghiz Khan were forbidden
to steal in time of peace. The penalty was death. Thus
many a western Christian friar and the remarkable Polos
(Marco, his father, and his uncle), among others, finally
became intimately acquainted with the ways of the East.

However, Jenghiz Khan never turned into a lovable
old patriarch. In 1226, the next-to-last year of his life,
he led his warriors on China again with the usual gory
victories. The next summer, having retired to Shan-si,
he was ravaged by fever. As he lay dying he turned to
a friend, Kiluken Bahadur.

"Be a true friend to Bortai," he said, "and to my sons
Ogotai and Tule. A man's body is not imperishable;
without a house or a resting place it decays . . . I must
take my leave of you and depart. The boy Kublai will
some day sit upon my throne and he will guard your
welfare as I have done." Before he died, Jenghiz put
his affairs in order, mapping out further campaigns against
China and dividing the empire among his five sons.

His body was secretly transported to Mongolia. No
advance news of his death preceded him; any one un-
lucky enough to meet the funeral cortege was slaughtered

Tartar warrior ready for battle

A medieval artist dramatized Jenghiz Khan's death this way. Actually he died in bed.

on the spot. Back among his people, the funeral ceremonies were awesome and tearful. But Bortai, his first and favorite wife, grieved in silence. A coffin, reputed to contain his bones, is still believed to lie in a heavily guarded ancient temple about fifty miles south of Lanchow, only a few miles from the first stage of the Silk Road.

For a time after Jenghiz's death, people of the West continued to live in terror. It seemed the Khan's successors would sweep through Europe and drive Christendom into the sea. But the Tartar wave shifted and swamped the Moslems. Could the Tartars be turned into allies? The word trickled back, too, that they were tolerant to many religions. Full of hope, missionaries and adventurers set out, cautiously, tentatively, hoping to learn about, trade with, and—who knew—maybe even convert to Christianity the wild horsemen of the East.

Friar John,
the First Adventurer

For the Italian monk Friar John of Pian de Carpine in Perugia, April 8, 1246, was hardly the usual Easter Sunday of Christian rejoicing. He and his companion, Friar Benedict the Pole, were not at all sure they would live to see the end of the day.

They were deep in the strange and inhospitable land of the Tartars, those savage nomads who had taken most of the world by sword. True, they were missionaries— the first of a new wave. Pope Innocent IV, newly elected and full of zeal, hoped to dissuade the Tartars from "their onslaughts on Christendom," to preach Christianity to them, and on the sly, to find out what invasion plans they had for Europe. Maybe, the Pope thought, the Khans could be converted. His hopes were raised by tales of a Christian kingdom believed to exist somewhere in the East, ruled by a legendary character known as "Prester John," and also by rumors that the Mongols worshiped a God.

Worthy though these motives were, they did little to ease Friar John's discomfort this Easter day. He and his companion were the first westerners to penetrate so far, and they were going farther still. That morning, weak from a Lenten diet of millet with salt and water, they had said Mass. Now, with two Tartar escorts at

A Tartar soldier

their sides, they were mounted on fast horses and gallop-
ing east, on a route north of and parallel to the Silk Road,
heading for Mongolia and the Great Khan himself. All
of this in the name of God.

The religious achievements of Friar John's mission were
not of great significance, but he did leave a legacy all
the same. His observant eye and attention to detail,
applied in a report to his Church superiors, gave us the
first truly well-rounded account of life in the time of the
Khans. This, then, was the kind of life that travelers
on the Silk Road were also experiencing.

A Nestorian monk

Friar John's mission was not the first trickle of faith
over the Silk Road. Centuries before other religions had
made inroads in China—notably Buddhism from India.
Buddhism too traveled over the trade route, first catching
on in Khotan, then spreading east until, by AD 300, there
were 3,700 monks and 180 Buddhist communities in
China.

Buddhism, with its doctrine of renunciation, chastity,
charity, and meekness, found greater acceptance in China
than any of the other immigrant religions. In urging
chastity the faith went counter to the Chinese belief
in the duty of procreation and this was the strong argu-
ment of Confucians versus Buddhists.

But the faith nevertheless became entrenched whereas
at least three others did not: Nestorianism, Zoroastrianism,
and Manichaeism. Nestorianism, a form of Christianity
shunned by traditional Christians, denied the divinity of
Christ and the holiness of the Virgin but included con-
cepts of Gospels, the Trinity, baptism, and the Cross,
new to the Chinese. It held a few followers until it
eventually withered away.

Zoroastrianism stressed the distinct opposition of good

Buddhist monasteries like this one afforded stopping places along the Silk Road.

to evil. It also offered some curious rules concerning fire: fire and water could not be allowed to touch; fire could not be soiled by having things thrown upon it or by being breathed upon; sunlight could not fall upon it. This faith had a fleeting foothold, as did Manichaeism, which preached that the spirit is good and matter is bad. It frowned on begetting children, treating illnesses, and feeding the human body.

So Friar John found himself among barbarians, already a year's distance away from Lyons and his native Italy, and God only knew how near to death or to a successful mission. Over the following weeks the bulky friar, who all his life had ridden nothing more spunky than a Franciscan donkey, found himself strapped to fast Tartar horses—he was provided with fresh mounts five to seven times a day—speeding across a bleak land of conquered people. His legs were wrapped in bandages to ease the pain and fatigue of riding. His morale was not improved by the sight of "human skulls and bones scattered about on the ground like cattle dung"—the same sight that filled many a Silk Road merchant with foreboding.

By late June the friar and his companion were in mountains, snowstorms, and extreme cold. On they rode, at the trot from dawn until dusk, into Mongolia. "Often we arrived so late that we did not eat at night but that which we should have eaten at night was given us in the morning," he wrote.

At last Friar John was at the Tartar camp, a half day's ride from the capital, Karakorum. There he saw sights never before witnessed by western eyes. He had arrived upon the eve of an auspicious occasion; a new emperor,

Kuyuk Khan probably had a yurt as elaborate as Jenghiz's (below).

Kuyuk Khan, a descendant of Jenghiz, was about to be
raised to the throne.

The coronation site was an enormous purple tent big
enough, the friars estimated, to hold 2,000. Around it,
as coronation day drew near, swarmed Tartar chieftains
in their finest velvets and silks of purple, red, and blue.
Even their horses looked elegant, with gold-trimmed
breastplates, saddles, and bits.

Two gates opened through the wooden palings around
the tent: one for the emperor only, the other for invited
guests. Unwanted visitors were beaten by guards or
shot down with arrows. While the common people
milled around in the distance the chiefs sat for hours,
drinking mare's milk and discussing the coronation.
They offered some milk to the friars, who could not
stomach the stuff.

The coronation was not for lowly eyes, but the friars
got a detailed description. With all the nobility of the
empire gathered around, Kuyuk was raised to a gold-
and-silver-encrusted throne. His followers placed a
sword before him and cried, "We want, we beg, and we
command that you shall have dominion over us."

"If you want me to reign over you," the Khan re-
sponded, "are you ready each one of you to do what I
shall command, to come whenever I call, to go wherever
I may choose to send you, to put to death whomsoever
I shall command you?"

"Yes!"

"My command shall be my sword!"

"Yes!"

They placed a piece of felt on the ground, seated the
Khan on it, and said, "Look upward and recognize God
and downward and see the felt on which you sit. If

Coronation of the Great Khan (fifteenth-century miniature)

you reign well over your kingdom, if you make largesse and rejoice in justice and honor each of your princes according to his rank, you shall reign in glory, all the world shall bow to your rule, and God will give you everything your heart can desire. But if you do otherwise you shall be miserable, lowly, and so poor that this felt on which you sit shall not even be left to you."

Then his chief wife came beside him and both were lifted high with loud cries acclaiming the emperor and empress of the Tartars.

Later the Khan was ensconced in a tent of silk and gold—pillars covered with gold plates, fastened with gold nails, top and sides of silk—while the multitude bowed down. Then the days of feasting and drinking began.

At last the visiting friars were conducted to the mighty leader, in company with other foreign ambassadors. An aide shouted their names aloud. Then each bent the left knee four times at the entrance. Tartar guards searched them for hidden knives.

"Do not tread upon the threshold as you enter," the Tartars warned. "He who knowingly treads on the emperor's threshold must die." And finally, entering the east door—never the sacred west door of the emperor himself—they found themselves in the presence of Kuyuk Khan.

They saw a man of medium stature, in his forties, solemn of face. He sat beneath an umbrella covered with precious stones, and was surrounded by gifts: plain silks, brocades, silk garments worked with gold, furs. Outdoors on a hillside more than 500 carts of gold, silver, and silken gowns waited to be divided among the Khan and his chiefs. The friars had no presents to offer; they could not possibly have matched such riches in any case.

It was an inconclusive visit. The Khan, neither then nor later, ever spoke to them directly. His custom with strangers was to listen as they spoke (always on their knees), then relay the answer, if any, through his chief "procurator," a man named Kadac. Kadac's words, in turn, were interpreted. On this day the Khan apparently said nothing.

There were many more tedious weeks of waiting. The friars and their Tartar guides were neither well nor badly treated. No one paid them special heed and they lived, Friar John recorded, "in such hunger and thirst that we were barely able to keep alive, for the allowances which

they gave the four of us were scarcely enough for one
and we could find nothing to buy, the market being too
far away."

At last, still communicating through intermediaries,
the Khan invited the friars to put down in writing the
nature of their mission. This was duly translated. Then
came the problem of getting the Khan's reply. Finally
his aides wrote their leader's remarks in Tartar and translated it aloud. The friars then composed their own
translation on the spot, checked it back and forth word
by word to avoid errors, and threw in another translation,
in Saracenic, for good measure.

Then on November 13, after four months in the land
of the Khan, the friars turned west. With them they
carried the letter bearing Kuyuk's seal, a fox-skin gown
for each, a gift from Kuyuk's mother, and a piece of
royal purple (from which the two Tartar guides each
promptly stole a bit).

The journey back in dead of winter was an ordeal.
Here, too, was a replica of the hardships suffered by
silk caravans.

"We were resting most of the time in the snow in the
desert," the friar wrote, "save when in the open plain,
where there were no trees, we could scrape a bare place
with our feet; and often when the wind drifted we
would find, on waking, our bodies all covered with
snow."

Weak and frostbitten, they made their way out of the
Tartar dominion, month by month, into the friendly
lands where "all came out to meet us rejoicing and con-
gratulated us as if we had risen from the dead." Everywhere they were plied with questions: what were the
Tartars like? What were their designs on the West?

Mongolian alphabet

Pope Alexander (above) sent Friar
John on a mission to the East.

In November, 1247, Friar John was home again, report-
ing to the Pope.   His mission had produced no momen-
tous results from the world political standpoint.   The
Khan's letter was haughty and vague; it neither opened
nor slammed the door to the East.   But Friar John had
survived, which was feat enough, and for it he was ap-
pointed to a bishopric.   Nonetheless, the ordeal had
ruined his health.   Five years later he died.

His legacy was inspiration and knowledge.   Specifi-
cally, his adventure inspired another quest by yet another monk, the doughty French-Flemish Friar William
of Rubruck, who soon went forth to collect an even
more meticulous account of life along the old Silk Road.

Who was Prester John?

Of all the real and imaginary wonders of the Silk Road —goblins, demons, barbarians, riches, thieves, and men of God—none was more puzzling, more elusive, or more naggingly persistent than the legend of Prester John. For some three centuries prior to the Middle Ages, his name cropped up continuously in tales and reports. Many sought him; a few claimed to have found him. Yet there is no evidence that Prester John was anything but a myth, made larger by the yearnings and yarnings of the travelers themselves, and perpetrated at least once by some mischievous unknown person. Even in the twentieth century, historians still take time to speculate about Prester John.

The first rumors of this legendary priest-king, ruling in the far away East, was circulated in the West by word of mouth. Early in the twelfth century came news of a great victory over the Persians by a "Johannes Presbyter." Again, tales were circulated concerning Prester John, a Nestorian king of fabulous wealth.

Then, about 1165, a letter reached Manuel I, Emperor of Byzantium, supposedly from Prester John himself. It filled in all the details that westerners yearned to hear, and it left no doubt that Prester John was a very big man in his own bailiwick.

A monk of the twelfth century

The powerful—but mythical—Prester John, John the Priest, was shown in a sixteenth-century book.

"I, Prester John, who reign supreme, surpass in virtue, riches, and power all creatures under Heaven," the letter modestly announced. "Seventy kings are our tributaries. I am a zealous Christian and universally protect the Christians of our empire, supporting them by our alms. We have determined to visit the sepulcher of our Lord with a very large army, in accordance with the glory of our majesty, to humble and chastise the enemies of the cross of Christ, and to exalt his blessed name."

According to the letter, Prester John's empire was a Hollywood version of paradise. Milk and honey literally flowed through the land. There were no "noisy frog croaks," no snakes, no scorpions. Through the heart of it flowed a river called the Indus, chock full of emeralds, sapphires, carbuncles, topazes, chrysolites, onyxes, beryls, and sardonyxes.

If Manuel I had any hope of throwing rank, either godly or military, at Prester John, his hopes withered as he read on. Prester's retinue included seven kings, sixty-two dukes, and 265 counts and marquises. Twelve archbishops sat at his right during meals, twenty bishops at his left.

Was Manuel wondering why God, having made Prester John "the most superpotential and most glorious over all mortals," did not give him a fancier title than "prester," which meant "priest"? Fear not, the letter assured. The court was full of many qualified ecclesiastics. "Our house steward is a patriarch and king; our chief cup bearer is an archbishop and king; our chamberlain is a bishop and king; our master of the horse is a king and abbot." So, out of sheer humility, Prester John had contented himself with the rank of "priest." But, the let-

An imaginary view of the fabled island kingdom of Prester John, believed to exist in the middle of India, sometimes in Ethiopia.

ter concluded, nobody should be misled by the humble title; "if you can number the stars of heaven and sands of the sea, then you may calculate the extent of our dominion and power."

It is hard to believe, now, that anyone could fall for such an obvious hoax. Years later the letter was acknowledged to be a forgery, although the practical joker was never discovered. But the twelfth-century western world desperately *wanted* to trust in a Prester John. He fitted in with everyone's longings for the existence of a never-never land that embodied all their dreams—an exotic East. They wanted to believe that easterners were not merely barbarians who hacked off people's heads. Their attitude toward Asians was somewhat like the modern movie fans' wistful view of their favorite stars: they hoped those people were God-fearing civilized folks like them, but more glamorous, more exciting. And so Prester John became the talk of Europe.

Pope Alexander III in 1177 heard that Prester John wanted to become a Catholic, so he sent off a letter via an emissary. The emissary, who had perpetrated the

rumor in the first place, was never seen again.   Prester
John was variously reported as King of Ethiopia and
King of India.   A fifteenth-century Italian book of po-
etry with fifty-nine verses devoted to him, pictures John
in the frontispiece: a firm-eyed venerable king with flowing robes and beard, a Bible on his knee, and on his
head a massive crown that would crush the average
man's skull.

For two and a half centuries the legend survived, and
Prester John was on every eastern traveler's list of people or things to find.

One such wanderer was Friar William of Rubruck.

Prester John in his glory is shown in a fifteenth-century book.

The Friar Who
Solved the Mystery
of the "Seres"

Fat Friar William of Rubruck, in French Flanders, was a man of several talents. First, he had the relentless determination of the missionary. In his 10,000-mile journey to Mongolia and back, beginning AD 1253, this middle-aged Franciscan was frozen, starved, and half-scared out of his wits, but he never considered turning back.

The western world was indebted to Friar William for much of what was known about the mysterious lands to the east. He was the first to identify the Chinese as the "Seres" of early Silk Road days and therefore the suppliers of "seric" cloth; he was also the first westerner to note that the Chinese used paper money, and one of the first to suspect that Prester John was pure myth.

Friar William was also a good reporter in other respects. His descriptions of Tartar life are, with Marco Polo's, the best in medieval literature. All in all, his was the most remarkable and productive journey up to that point in the long history of the Silk Road.

The friar was the unofficial emissary of King Louis IX of France. Both he and the king were excited and encouraged by Friar John's safe return from the East. For William, as for many missionaries after him, John's example was an inspiration. It was a challenge, almost a

Louis IX sent Friar William to Asia.

duty, for other men of God to visit those remote places, preach the faith, and win souls for the Church of Rome.

King Louis, for his part, was eager to assess the powerful Tartars' plans and motives, without committing himself to anything. Were they a threat to western Europe? The king wanted to know, but without letting the Tartars know he was concerned.

Accordingly, Friar William set out with letters of recommendation to the Tartar rulers, a small sum of money from the king, an illuminated psalter from the queen, a Bible from the king, his breviary, and a few

devotional books.   He lingered in Constantinople to
stock up on fruits, muscatel wine, and dainty biscuits.
On May 7, William, a fellow friar, and five men struck
out for the East on horseback, hauling their supplies in
oxcarts.   Like Friar John, they did not cling to the Silk
Road route; but in every respect except geography, the
sights they saw and the life they lived was that of contemporary caravaners.

On June 3, William met his first Tartars.   With lively
curiosity he recorded their ways in intimate detail: their
wandering life from winter lowlands to high summer
pasture lands, their portable tents or "yurts," and the
strict rules of etiquette governing who sat where in a
Tartar yurt.   He noticed that Tartars of high rank had
several wives and "she with whom he hath slept that
night sits beside him in the day and it becometh all the
others to come to her dwelling that day to drink and
court is held there that day and gifts which are brought
that day are placed in the treasury of that lady.   A
bench with a skin of milk or some other drink, with
cups, stands in the entry."

He watched their merry-making and observed that in

Tartars of the Mongol era
(above and opposite page)

Page from Bible sent by Louis IX to
the Khan

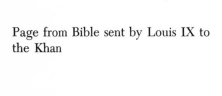

winter the Tartars made "a capital drink of rice, millet, and of honey; it is clear as wine." In summer they drank only *cosmos*, a fermented mare's milk. There was shouting, singing, and dancing to guitars, and "when they want to challenge anyone to drink they take hold of him by the ears and pull so as to distend his throat, and they clap and dance before him."

The men were rough, rude warriors, clad during winter in two fur gowns of wolf or fox, one with the fur against the body, the other with fur to the outside. Breeches, too, were of fur and, for the rich, lined with soft, light, warm silk wadding. The poor made do with dogskin gowns and cotton linings.

"The women," Friar William later reported to this king, "are wonderfully fat, and she who has the least nose is held the most beautiful. They disfigure themselves horribly by painting their faces. They never lie down in bed when having their children."

Such were the people that surrounded the friar's party one June day. For a long time they made the travelers squat in the shade of their carts while the Tartars looked them over.

"Have you ever been among us before?" one finally asked.

"Never."

"Give us something to eat and drink."

The friar reluctantly parted with some biscuits and a flagon of wine, which the Tartars gulped down.

"Give us more," demanded a Tartar. "A man enters not a house with one foot only."

Friar William refused; his stock was low.

"Where do you come from and where do you want to go?"

Tartars rode oxen as well as horses.

"I have letters to Sartach." This was the Mongol chief in the area.

"Do you come of your own free will or were you sent?"

"No one forced me," said the friar stoutly, careful to not represent himself as an official ambassador, "nor would I go if I did not want to."

"Have you gold and silver for Sartach in the carts?"

"Sartach will see for himself," said the friar sharply. "It is none of your business. Now show me to your captain, and if it please him, he shall have me taken to Sartach. If not we shall go back."

The Tartars finally agreed, but not before badgering the friar with pleas for bread, knives, belts, and gloves, and jeers that he was an imposter. How many hundreds of Silk Road caravans must have undergone the same harassment—a fairly harmless but frightening test of nerves.

"It seemed to me that we had escaped from the midst of the devils," was the good friar's comment when they finally left. A day later William won permission to see Sartach. In the next two months the friar and his party slept every night in the open air, under the carts if it were raining. He learned to drink cosmos. "I broke out in sweat with horror and surprise. It seemed to me, however, very palatable." This was lucky because, although the mild intoxicant was perhaps not a holy man's drink, it was usually the only liquid available.

He often was near starvation. With a guide the party was now up to eight. There was never enough food, and in each populated stopping place, crowds pressed in on them "to the point of crushing us in their eagerness to see all our things. If they were seized with a desire to void their stomachs they did not go away from us farther than one can throw a bean."

On July 31, they reached Sartach's camp, and after the usual preliminaries with the hangers-on, were admitted to the great man. Friar William put on his finest vestments, and with Bible and psalter, greeted the chieftain, his six wives, and his court. King Louis's letters were gravely accepted, as were more gifts from the friar's seemingly inexhaustible supply of fruit and wine. They withdrew in good order.

But in the morning an aide arrived with new orders: Sartach felt unqualified to answer the King's letters; he was passing the buck to his father, Batu. The friar must go on to see him. Some of William's belongings were temporarily impounded; some were never returned!

The friar went on, disgruntled with Sartach, whose hospitality and religious tolerance seemed to be in direct ratio to the gifts his visitors brought. Not once in the four days had the chieftain offered food. On the next leg of the journey Friar William existed on biscuits. To heighten the discomfort of the journey, the little party

Friar William may have been in a Tartar village which looked like this.

moved in constant fear of gangs of runaway slaves who
lurked in the woods by day and plundered by night.

In September they reached the camp of Batu. This
chieftain, reclining on a couch with his henchmen around
him, listened to their story and offered them some cosmos, which the friar was beginning to like. Batu was
friendly, but he could not let them stay in the country
without clearing it with Mangu, the Great Khan in
Mongolia.

For five weeks William and his party stayed with
Batu's camp. "Sometimes my companion was so hungry
that he would say to me almost with tears in his eyes,
'It seems to me I shall never get anything to eat.' The
market always follows the [horde] of Batu, but it was
so far away from us that we could not get there for we
had to travel afoot." Some friendly Hungarians finally
helped out with a little meat.

At last a Tartar came to them with news.

"I am to take you to Mangu Khan. The journey is a

Friar William of Rubrick
reached the Court of Batu.

four months' one and it is so cold that stones and trees are split by the cold. Think over whether you can bear it."

"I trust that by the grace of God we may be able to bear what other men can bear," said Friar William.

"If you cannot bear it," the Tartar sneered, "I shall abandon you on the road."

"That is not right. We are not going of ourselves but are sent for by your lord. So, being entrusted to your care, you should not abandon us."

It was a shrewd rebuttal. The Tartar lost his swagger. "All will be well," he promised. The next day he supplied the friars with sheepskin gowns, breeches, boots, felt stockings, and hoods.

For months they rode, changing mounts two or three times a day when possible. "They always gave me a strong horse on account of my great weight. But I dared not inquire whether he rode easily or not, nor did I venture to complain if he proved hard, but had to bear it all with equal good grace. Consequently we used to have to endure extreme hardships. Oftimes the horses were tired out before we had reached the stage and we had to beat and whip them, put our clothing on other pack horses, change our saddle horses for pack horses, and sometimes even the two of us ride one horse."

They were hungry and thirsty almost constantly. The Tartars gave out food only in the evening: mutton and some pot liquor, the meat generally half-raw because of a shortage of ox or horse dung fuel for cooking. Breakfast was never more than a few mouthfuls of millet gruel. Now and again along the way William had his moments regaling the people with tales of Europe, assuring them that the Pope was really *not* 500 years old as they thought, and awing them with the flat statement that the "Ocean sea is endless, without bounds!" Always he was plagued by inadequate or inaccurate interpreters, which he became aware of as he grasped a little of the language himself.

Despite his physical discomfort, William was soaking up much knowledge of the East. He kept voluminous notes on the way of life and beliefs, especially on "great Cathay whose people were anciently called Seres. From among them come the best silk stuffs which are called 'seric' by that people. . . . These Cathayans are small men who in speaking aspirate strongly through the nose, and in common with all Orientals have small openings for the eyes."

On November 30, the party reached a village of Nestorians. The friars' joy was almost pathetic: "We entered their church singing joyfully 'Salve regina!' for it had been a long time since we had seen a church."

On again—would the journey never end?—they rode into towering mountains which perhaps were the home of some of the demons who dogged the ancient travelers of the Silk Road.

On December 13, a Sunday, as they passed through a fierce rocky gorge, the guide sent back a panicky plea.

"We beg you to say some prayers that will put the devils to flight. In this gorge they will carry men off. Sometimes they seize only the horse. Sometimes they tear out the rider's bowels and leave the body on the horse!"

A Tartar school

The friars chanted heartily as they rode, the little band came through unscathed, and from then on Friar William's stock was higher with the guide. Any man who could drive off mountain devils must be powerful.

Tartar silk culture

At the end of December, after nearly four months on the road, they reached the Khan's camp. As usual, the welcome was not overwhelming. The guide was assigned a large tent; the friars got a pitiful hut. Their diet was the familiar millet broth with a little meat; the guide went to a feast and got drunk. Friar William tried going barefoot in the manner of his order and froze the tips of his toes.

Again he went through the familiar ritual of being presented to a noble Tartar. This time, the audience had comic-opera overtones. In celebration of the Nativity he and his companion led off with a hymn. Then the guards searched them from head to toe for knives and admitted them to a house lined with gold cloth, where a fine roaring fire of briars and cattle dung burned. There lounged Mangu Khan, a small man of forty-five in a glossy otter-skin garment, with a young wife and assorted children including "a very ugly full-grown girl called Cirina." The Khan offered them a choice of drinks: rice wine, cosmos, or honey mead.

"My lord," said the friar piously, "We are not men who seek to satisfy our fancies about drinks. Whatever pleases you will suit us." The Khan passed around rice wine, and soon the guide-interpreter was drunk again.

Hunting falcon

The Khan played with his hunting falcons for a while, then bade the friars drop to their knees and speak.

Friar William repeated his familiar story—the messages from France, the apologies for having no fine gifts (they were, after all, only poor priests), and finally a plea that they be allowed to remain a while until they recovered their strength.

The Khan listened gravely and replied through an intermediary. "As the sun sends its rays everywhere, likewise my sway and that of Batu reaches everywhere, so we do not want your gold or silver." At this point the interpreter grew so drunk, and Mangu himself a trifle tipsy, that the translation became incoherent. Conversation petered out and the audience ended. But later the word came down: the friars could stay two months, until the cold had passed, and could also go on to the capital, Karakorum, if they wished.

"May the Lord keep Mangu Khan and give him a happy and long life!" cried Friar William.

They continued to be cold and hungry until they moved in with a Nestorian monk who had managed to find better quarters. Men of many faiths lingered around Mangu's camp. This one, it turned out, was a fraud— a cloth weaver posing as a holy man, and practising a kind of faith-healing. His favorite cure was holy water mixed with rhubarb. The Tartars were mightily impressed with the sheer power of this purgative, until one day the dose nearly killed a sick boy. Friar William scolded the false monk and threatened to expose him.

So the weeks passed, in jockeying with men of other religions, trying to get a chance to convert the Khan, and picking up all manner of lore. William described paper money "of cotton, in length and breadth a palm, and on it they stamp lines like those on the seal of Mangu." He observed Chinese writing "with a brush such as painters paint with, and they make in one figure the several letters containing a whole word."

In May he visited Karakorum, where the Khan held court. The friar was unimpressed. He grumbled that the city was not even as big as Saint Denis, a suburb of Paris. However, his account is worth noting because Karakorum must have been typical of the cities along the Silk Road. Inasmuch as it was only slightly north of the northernmost leg of the Road around the Gobi Desert, many caravaners probably visited Karakorum itself.

Chinese characters were often inscribed on silk.

"There are two quarters in it," reported Friar William. "One, of the Saracens, in which are the markets and where a great many Tartars gather on account of the court which is always near this city, and on account of the great number of ambassadors. The other is the quarter of the Cathayans, all of whom are artisans."

William also reported "twelve idol temples of different nations," two mosques, and one Christian church. This was a fair representation of the religious tolerance permitted under the Khans.

Most interesting was William's report on the markets, typical of Asian towns. "The city is surrounded by a mud wall and has four gates. At the eastern is sold millet and other kinds of grain. At the western one, sheep and goats are sold. At the southern, oxen and carts are sold. At the northern, horses are sold." Life was good for the people of Karakorum. Every day, 500 cart loads of food and drink rolled in from different parts of the empire.

Western artist's idea of Tartar village

Friar William must have been a little astonished when in late May, after he had been there nearly five months, he received this message: "Mangu Khan wishes to know why you have come to these parts."

"He must know from Batu's letters!"

"The letters have been lost and he has forgotten what Batu wrote in them."

So the friar explained it all over again. By various relays of messages Mangu let it be known that he wished Friar William well but it was time he went home. Before they left, however, there would be a great debate of the faiths: Christians, Nestorians, and all the Asiatic religions. This time Friar William had a reliable interpreter.

The debate waged back and forth before an appreciative audience, including representatives of the Khan. Friar William held his own but, as he wistfully wrote his king later, "No one said, 'I believe, I want to become a Christian.'" Afterward there was singing; then some of the holy men got drunk.

A few days later Friar William had his last audience with Mangu. The Khan was friendly but still sitting firmly on the middle of the religious fence.

"We believe there is only one God by whom we live

and by whom we die and for whom we have an upright heart. But as God gives us the different fingers of the hand, so he gives to me divers ways. God gives you the scriptures and you Christians keep them not. You do not find in them, for example, that one should find fault with another, do you?"

"No, my lord, but I told you from the first that I did not want to wrangle with anyone."

"Likewise you do not find that a man should depart from justice for money?"

"No, my lord, and truly I came not to these parts to obtain money; on the contrary I have refused what has been offered to me." A secretary present confirmed that Friar William had consistently rejected rich gifts.

"I do not say it of you," agreed the Khan. "God gave you therefore the scriptures and you (Christians) do not keep them. He gave us diviners, we do what they tell us, and we live in peace."

So they parted and Friar William began the long tortuous journey home. Almost one year later to the day he was back at Tripoli. He had won no converts or even real friends in the inscrutable East but he knew it as no other westerner did, and knew how to record his knowledge so that it would be passed on.

Marco Polo

By the middle of the thirteenth century, the importance of the Silk Road, as such, was fading. It carried as many spices, furs, chests of tea, and cargoes of porcelain as it did silks. But the old road had one more moment of glory: it carried the traveler Marco Polo who, until our century, was the most diligent observer and recorder of Asian life in all history.

It was an ideal time for the adventurer. The Silk Road had never been safer. The Tartar Empire, so thoroughly and properly condemned for its brutality, nevertheless did the world an enormous service by clearing a direct path between East and West and policing it reasonably well. Of the many who traveled it, none so thoroughly did it justice as Polo. He was, indeed, the last European to record a journey on the Silk Road. Soon after he passed over it, the Road and China were closed to the world and remained so for centuries. When at last they opened again, both had changed irrevocably.

Although Marco Polo made the history, his father, Nicolo, and his uncle, Maffeo, were responsible for his fame. About the time William of Rubruck made his journey east, the older Polos, Venetian jewel merchants, were on a trading expedition to the Khan of the Golden

Polo brothers, Marco's father and uncle, leave Venice on first journey to the little-known East.

Polo brothers appear before Kublai Khan as monks.

Horde on the Volga. They spent a year there. Then they found that a war had cut off their route home so they light-heartedly turned east instead.

They duly found themselves in China in the presence of Kublai, the great Khan, grandson of Jenghiz. He welcomed them, listened to their tales of the West, and finally sent them back, bearing two requests to the Pope. Kublai asked for one hundred learned men to preach to his Tartars and he also wanted some oil from the sacred lamp on the sepulcher in Jerusalem.

The brothers picked their way back (it took three years), obtained letters from Pope Gregory X and holy oil, but found only two holy men willing to face the rigors of the trail. These two panicked and fled, early on the return trip in 1271.

But with them they had someone of much more value to the Khan: Nicolo's son, nineteen-year-old Marco. Marco was to serve the Khan for seventeen years. More

In Constantinople, Polo brothers appear before Emperor.

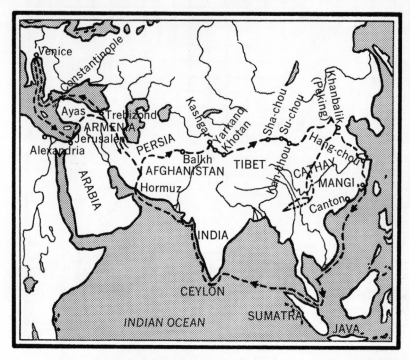

Marco Polo visited the Khan and remained to serve him for seventeen years. Map shows route of his journey.

important for us, he applied his inquisitive eye and passion for detail to everything he saw. He rambled freely around Asia. He learned several languages. Although at times his objectivity was clouded when eulogizing the Tartars, Marco's is an invaluable report on Asian life in the last days of the Silk Road.

The Polos started in the footsteps of the old caravaners at Balkh, moved on through the Pamirs, and followed that famous Kashgar-Yarkan-Khotan section along the Takla Makan, into the Gobi, along the Great Wall, and so to Kanbalu (Peking).

Marco left his history in the form of small vignettes. Samarkand he described as "a noble city, adorned with beautiful gardens, and surrounded by a plain, in which are produced all the fruits that man can desire." It had apparently recovered from the onslaughts of Jenghiz Khan.

Nicolo and Maffeo Polo, the father and uncle of Marco Polo, bid
farewell to Kublai Khan.

Kashgar, the terminus at the west end of the Takla Makan, still seemed to be a thriving commercial center. Polo reported handsome gardens, orchards, and vineyards, and noted the production of cotton, hemp, and flax.

"Merchants from this country travel to all parts of the world," Polo said, "but in truth they are a covetous, sordid race, eating badly and drinking worse."

In Yarkand, Polo found many people afflicted with goiter, as did travelers seven centuries later. This was apparently caused by deficiencies in local water and diet and may have been a common sight to travelers of the Silk Road in earliest times.

At Khotan he found "everything necessary for human life." Here, one of the great stopping places for silk caravans and the place where the legendary princess brought the first stolen secrets of silk, were farms and vineyards—cotton, flax, hemp, grain, and wine.

In this part of Asia as in many others, Polo found the sexual customs fairly permissive. "If a married man goes to a distance from home to be absent twenty days, his wife has a right, if she is inclined, to take another husband. The men, on the same principle, marry wher-

The three Polos depart from Venice. (They are shown by Grand Canal, in small boat, and then in galley.)

Title page of first printed edition of *Travels of Marco Polo*, 1477

ever they happen to reside." Farther along he discovered a custom whereby a stranger, arriving from a hard day on the trail, was offered every privilege of the home, including access to wives, sisters, and daughters. Men of the house, in fact, moved out to let the stranger have free rein. The courtesy was supposed to please the deities and bring down blessings on the house.

"The women," Polo said, "are in truth very handsome, very sensual, and full disposed to conform in this respect at the injunction of their husbands." According to history, he added, Mangu Khan once banned this custom of woman-sharing, but the inhabitants reported such bad crops and general misfortune as a result that the Khan said, "Since you appear so anxious to persist in your own shame and ignominy, let it be granted as you desire. Go, live according to your base customs and manners, and let your wives continue to receive the beggarly wages of their prostitution."

At Lop Nor the Polos prepared to cross the Gobi Desert. This was a route that the Silk Road did not take (it usually skirted the western edge of that desert), but it involved the same desert preparations and perils that faced the ancient caravaners of the Takla Makan. Polo

From *Travels of Marco Polo*

Portrait of Kublai Khan painted on silk

dwells not at all on physical hardships, but he was fascinated by the demons and goblins.

"If, during the daytime, any person remain behind on the road, either when overtaken by sleep or detained by their natural occasions, until the caravan has passed a hill and is no longer in sight, they unexpectedly hear themselves called by their names and in a tone of voice to which they are accustomed."

So, he said, these unfortunates were led away, lost, and left to die. At night the travelers might hear the

march of a large cavalcade nearby, would hurry to join
it, and again would end up alone and wandering. Sometimes, according to Polo, the ghosts took human form:
"These spirits assume the appearance of their traveling
companions, who address them by name and endeavor
to conduct them out of the proper road. It is said also
that some persons, in their course across the desert, have
seen what appeared to be a body of armed men advanc-
ing toward them and, apprehensive of being attacked
and plundered, have taken flight."

Reports of the eerie wailing of musical instruments
and the mystical throbbing of drums persisted, too.
Polo carefully avoided saying that *he* witnessed any
evidences of the supernatural. Probably all of the stories
could be explained in terms of wind, sandstorm noises,
mirages, or illusions brought on by heat, fatigue, and the
fear which grew over the centuries. But no matter; the
spirits of the desert were real enough to travelers and
enhanced the actual terror of their journey.

In some cases Polo's accuracy faltered. He was confident that he had tracked down the Prester John legend,
and that the latter was in fact a legendary prince named
Un-khan, who was killed in battle with Jenghiz Khan.
Jenghiz himself was pictured as a benevolent and lovable
leader; Polo (perhaps prudently, since he was working
for Jenghiz's grandson) skated carefully around the atroc-
ity stories.

Subsequently, as he settled in the Khan's court, Polo
had nothing but the best to say of Kublai. Other reports and drawings of the Khan show a fat Oriental face,
with pointed black beard and villainous pointed black
moustache. To Polo, Kublai was "of middle stature . . .
his limbs well formed and in his whole feature there is

Marco Polo's galley in which he left on first leg of his travels

a just proportion. His complexion is fair and occasionally suffused with red, like the bright tint of the rose, which adds much grace to his countenance."

Nevertheless, allowing for a certain amount of bias, Polo's accounts of life at court and in the cities of the ruler are full of fascinating lore. Like his grandfather, Kublai ran his own private beauty contest every year. His agents picked some 500 young beauties from around the kingdom and rated them on a point system of "sixteen carats" and up, based on the quality of hair, eyes, eyebrows, lips, and other points of interest. Anything of twenty carats or more went to Kublai.

They were then shipped in parties of five to the Khan's quarters, for three day-and-night shifts where, as Polo discreetly put it, "He does with them as he likes."

As Polo became acquainted with China, his writings increasingly mentioned silk—silk clothing, silk manufacture, silk trade. The capital city of Kanbalu was a place of twelve gates, populous suburbs (which were inhabited by 25,000 prostitutes, among others), the Khan's palace, and traders from all over the world.

"To this city everything that is most rare and valuable in all parts of the world finds its way; and more especially does this apply to India, which furnishes precious stones, pearls, and various drugs and spices. . . . The quality of merchandise sold there exceeds also the traffic of any other place; for no fewer than a thousand carriages and packhorses loaded with raw silk make their daily entry; and gold tissues and silks of various kinds are manufactured to an enormous extent."

Here, too, was the royal mint where, the adoring Marco believed, the Khan had "the secret of the alchemists, as he has the art of producing money." What the Khan's men did was strip bark from the mulberry trees, peel off its thin inner rind, soak it, reduce it to pulp, turn it into paper, and then into money.

In his seventeen years of service Polo saw and described much more. He had unprecedented access to remote corners of Asia. He traveled through a number of Chinese provinces, skirted the edge of Tibet, penetrated into northern Burma. He was for three years governor of the Chinese city of Yangchow. He produced a detailed account of the Khan's summer residence at Shandu, with marble palace, bamboo pavilion, woods, gardens, white mares, and magicians. Long after, the poet Coleridge drew from Polo for a famous verse:

> "In Xanadu did Kubla Khan
> A stately pleasure dome decree . . ."

Polo visited ports where junks sailed majestically to and fro with tons of pepper, spices, ebony, jewels, Tibetan musk, and, of course, Chinese silk. When at last he returned to Europe in 1295 he had seen sights no westerner had ever seen or *would* ever see, for Asia was soon to be torn apart once more.

The "Roc," a mythical giant bird which fed its young on elephants, was described by Marco Polo.

Once There Was
a Traveling Salesman...

For a few years after Polo, other westerners, making the most of the Tartars' leniency, flooded into Asia. The Silk Road was no longer a major channel for silk. The distance was a disadvantage; trade was becoming highly competitive, and carrying charges were a decisive factor. But the still-precious stuff was continuing to move.

The route, as always through the ages, was changing to cope with the shifting pattern of warring nations. At the beginning of the fourteenth century, the favorite trail extended from the Crimea to Tana (Azov) just east of the Black Sea, then ran around the northern end of the Caspian Sea, and south between the Caspian and the Aral Sea to Bokhara. Here it picked up the old route to the East via Samarkand.

Right up until the collapse of East-West communications again, the road was important. In fact, some sources say that it was by way of the Silk Road that the Black Death found its way to Europe from China in bales of silk, about 1348.

With every caravan traveled traders, forerunners of the traveling salesman. They carried wares to the East, where they traded them for others which they brought back to the West. Like salesmen everywhere, they were a unique breed. History has left us a glimpse of one:

the incomparable Francesco Balducci Pegolotti, merchant of the Bardi Company, Florence.

About 1340, Pegolotti wrote a remarkable book. It was a treatise on what every trader should know if he were planning to make the long journey from Tana to Cathay and to return with silk "to the value of 25,000 golden florins." Comparisons are dangerous but, very approximately, this might be equal to $50,000 or $60,000. Inadvertently, through the book, Pegolotti tells us much of himself. He was a gregarious soul, full of huckster's wisdom, a decent show of piety, and an endless array of small facts. Want to know where to stay, where to eat, and what to pay along the Silk Road? Ask Francesco Balducci Pegolotti.

The book was entitled *In the Name of the Lord, Amen!*, which suggests that the shrewd Pegolotti was

The Tartar palace in Peking has changed little over the years.

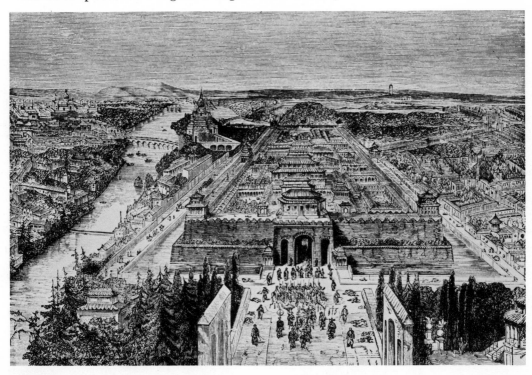

hedging his bets.   He was the fourteenth-century Elmer
Gantry; it could not hurt a drummer to have the Lord
and the Church on his side.   Before he got down to hard
facts, Pegolotti included a bit of homely doggerel; he
was also the fourteenth-century Edgar Guest:

"Honesty is always best
And to look before ye leap.
Do ever what thou promisest
And hard though it may be, still keep
Fair chastity.   Let reason tell
Cheap to buy and dear to sell,
But have a civil tongue as well.
Frequent the church's rites, and spare
To Him who sends thy gains a share.
So shalt thou prosper, standing by one price
And shunning pest-like usury and dice
Take aye good heed to govern well thy pen
And blunder not in black and white!   Amen!"

Silk was transferred to other caravans at terminals such as Samarkand and Tashkent.

Then the jolly salesman got down to specifics: what routes to take (basically, the aforementioned trail out of Tana and by way of Samarkand, then north around the Takla Makan to China); what beasts to use (oxen or horses, then camels and mules, depending on the terrain); the various weights and measures the trader would encounter along the way (everything from the "great pound" and the "little pound" to "tocchetto" and "aspers"—a whole host of terms foreign to our modern world). The journey, one-way, in Pegolotti's careful breakdown, took about 284 days.

Pegolotti urged merchants to take along linens to be sold; flour and salt fish to supplement such provisions as they would be able to acquire along the way; and silver which would be translated into paper money in Cathay. He reckoned that one somno of silver (a silver ingot, equivalent to five gold florins in the English currency of that time) would buy nineteen to twenty pounds of Cathay silk, or three to three and one-half pieces of damask silk, or three and one-half to five pieces of silk and gold fabric.

Pegolotti, for all his God-fearing verse, was not above handing out bribes along the way. "Don't forget that if you treat the customs house officers with respect and make them something of a present in goods or money, as well as their clerks and dragomen [guide interpreters], they will behave with great courtesy and always be ready to appraise your wares below their real value."

He had a few other general tips.

"In the first place," he advised, "you must let your beard grow long and not shave. And at Tana you should furnish yourself with a dragoman, and you must not try to save money in the matter of dragomen by taking a

Western idea of what Orientals looked like (sixteenth century)

Chinese scroll concerning
export of silk (1452)

bad one instead of a good one, for the additional wages
of the good one will not cost you so much as you will
save by having him.   And besides the dragoman it will
be well to take at least two good men servants who are
acquainted with the Cumanian tongue.   The road you
travel from Tana to Cathay is perfectly safe whether by
day or by night, according to what the merchants say
who have used it. . . .''

"Perfectly safe."   In a way, this is the most astonish-
ing comment in Pegolotti's book—one which would have
amazed the Silk Road traders of old.   Perhaps it indi-
cated to what degree law and order had been maintained under the ruthless rule of the Tartars.   But this
comfortable state of affairs would soon vanish.   For in
that year, 1340, a certain Mongol boy, Timur, was four
years old and quickly growing to manhood.   Timur
was soon to be known as Tamerlane the Conqueror,
Tamerlane the Terrible.

Road's End

In career and temperament the boy Timur was strikingly
like another nomad conqueror, Jenghiz Khan. Each was
unspeakably savage yet each, in his brutal way, was an
able ruler with a talent for administration and the
meting out of a kind of rough justice.

Timur was the last of the nomad kings to overrun the
world. And, ruthless though he was, he was simply a
logical product of his times. He was born on April 9,
1336, in an oasis valley not far from Samarkand on the
Silk Road. He was the son of a certain Taraghay, of a
Mongol clan that had melted into the Tartar empire.
He grew up like most boys of his time, struggling for
survival. Having become an excellent horseman and
archer, he headed a bandit force of well-armed riders
who lived by raiding neighboring lands and caravans.

At about age twenty-seven he was crippled in battle.
For the rest of his life Timur was physically marked,
an unforgettable figure with a name that at first was
shouted with scorn and later was whispered with terror:
Timur i leng, "Timur the Lame," eventually "Tamerlane."

Like many leaders, he was bigger than the average
man of his time and race—about five foot seven, lean
and muscular, with high cheekbones, a slight Oriental

Timur, last great nomad
conqueror

cast to the eyes, a cruel mouth, and reddish hair, beard, and moustache. The wounds left his right arm and hand withered, but still functioning and strong. His right thigh had grown fast at the hip. This leg was shorter than the other, causing a severe limp. Nevertheless he could walk and could spend days on end in the saddle. In later life, servants carried him to his horse or bullock cart.

Tamerlane early discovered the art of murder. At age twenty-five he ruled a small rich area. He formed an alliance with a neighboring ruler, Emir Husayn, and married Husayn's sister. Together they extended their holdings. But they quarreled increasingly, and finally Tamerlane marched on his brother-in-law, captured him, had him killed by a henchman, and took over his kingdom and his wives.

Other conquests quickly followed. His adoring people moved with him. The hordes of warriors were accompanied by women and children, flocks and herds. The women joined their men in battle. Often, men in Tamerlane's armies had been born on the trail where their warrior mothers fought alongside their fathers. They grew to manhood and started families of their own, without ever having a permanent home.

Tamerlane inherited the "tuman" (ten thousand) unit system of army organization from the Khans, in which each unit of ten had its own commander, each ten commanders had a chief, and so on. Every soldier was well equipped with a bow, thirty arrows, and a shield. Every two horsemen had a spare mount between them; every ten were required to have a tent, two spades, a pick-axe, a scythe, an awl, an axe, one hundred needles, and a cooking pot.

Timur gets ready for battle.

بیشاه نطر بنمایت بسیاری روی ما بنها ذند و شمشیرهای خون آشام آنیام انتقام برآورده و غو کشیدندو یک دفعه کو که
و نعار غزو کونند و همه در زمان از طرف بالا آب اسپ زاده میر انشاه و اسپ زاده شامرخ و اسپ سلیمان انشاه و دیکر
ابرای تومان و مان در صف وصف و از دیکر طرف اسپ زاده رستم و امیر شاملک و بندو علی سلطان و بسیار امرای متور و حکام ملک کدر
و دیوانهای حصار تا حمله در نمند و عساکر دو نثار از اطراف و جوانب بشهر در آمدند و سپاهیان را مصد قلمهه نرسبه السمیا
شاهدی افنادو نضر تصاحب حضر بر آن روی در آن روی و نثر آمد خبر و مود دکر حسب و مان غزاز نبینه داد عظیم

European concept of Tartars (sixteenth century)

The richer and greater warriors had single-edged swords with sharp curved points, pointed helmets, and coats of mail. Some chiefs also wore a sleeveless velvet jacket, lined or covered on the outside with scales of metal discs. The ordinary soldier wore a leather suit but no armor, and carried a file to sharpen his arrowheads, which cut both ways like a double-edge sword.

Aside from their personal equipment, Tamerlane's armies used all the latest killing devices, such as containers or grenades filled with naphtha to burn down enemy defenses, fire arrows made by fixing slow-burning gunpowder to arrowheads, and stones projected by gunpowder explosions. The engineers built pontoon bridges of rafts or reeds over those fierce rivers that were too much even for the swashbuckling horsemen.

Coupled with this equipment in the hands of excellent warriors was Tamerlane's sheer cunning. He alone assessed each campaign and made the decisions. Trickery was one of his most valuable weapons. He favored a darting attack, then a sudden shift to another quarter altogether. This kept his opponents confused, off balance. An enemy could never count on Tamerlane to fight by the rules. Adversaries also learned to distrust everything they heard or saw.

As head of a kingdom, Tamerlane employed the same tactics. In the early days before he had accumulated an empire, he routed a superior enemy force, first by lighting a multitude of campfires at night, suggesting a huge army, then during the day by attaching branches to the flanks of his 200 horses and stirring up enough dust for 2,000. The enemy literally fled from a cloud of dust. He received a party of envoys from a khan who demanded that the Tartar submit or prepare for battle. When the

Westernized concept of Timur, ruler of over fifteen million people

emissaries arrived, Tamerlane suddenly turned aside and vomited blood. The agents went back reasurred: old Timur the Lame was too sick to cause any trouble. But the blood was that of a wild boar—Tamerlane had swallowed a basin full just before they arrived—and in short order, he overran them.

When a battle was over Tamerlane strictly controlled the pillaging. It was not that he disapproved, for booty from the spoils of battle was necessary to the Tartars' survival. Everything was taken—gold, furs, corn, arms, and people. But the hordes had to wait for the signal, a black banner hoisted over the camp. Soldiers who disobeyed were cut down.

Plunder was shared in an orderly fashion and according to rank. Tamerlane was a generous cutthroat; he knew that his warriors wanted food, riches, and women and he saw that all of their appetites were appeased.

Such was the well-organized and generally devoted throng that followed Tamerlane on his trail of conquest. By 1380 he had subjugated most of the Tartar regions and turned on Persia. He marched on the city of Khorasan. The plains surrounding the city were thick with tents, banners, horsemen, foot soldiers. Drums thundered, seven-foot trumpets blared at dawn, and the townspeople surrendered in fear at the sights and sounds alone.

It was just as well; most of them got off by paying a heavy ransom. Cities that resisted were treated to the sight of towers built with the heads of the slain. When the town of Isfizar rose up in revolt, Tamerlane built an even more grisly tower—2,000 captives were piled one atop the other, still alive, and cemented with layers of clay and brick. This was a stern warning against any

other insurrection. At the city of Zaranj, Tamerlane's
horse was shot from under him. In punishment, the
walls were razed to the ground and every person slaughtered. Zaranj literally disappeared from the map.

In 1386–87, the conqueror moved from Persia to take
Iraq, Azerbaijan, and Armenia. After one of the victories
the troops celebrated with a typical hunt. They en-
circled a large wooded area and herded every living
thing together. Tamerlane and his nobility had first
crack at the game; the soldiers followed in order of
rank. There was enough for everyone—too much, in
fact. They left behind heaps of dead stags, does, tigers,
and other game for beasts and birds of prey.

After every campaign, Tamerlane retired to Samarkand, his headquarters. Here he and his men luxuriated
in the spoils: eating, drinking, womanizing. At such
orgies, thousands of guests gorged themselves on all
kinds of meat, including entire roast horses, and gulped
wine from golden beakers. Ladies paraded in silk, velvet, and satin robes heavy with gold lace and with trains
so long that fifteen maidservants had to carry them.

Tartar ladies followed
their men from camp to
camp.

FEMINE TARTARICI.

The conqueror himself indulged sparingly in these delights. He was a serious, almost glum figure, with a furiously active mind. Although not especially literate, he surrounded himself with scholars and held his own when matching wits with them. He valued practical knowledge of medicine, astronomy, and mathematics. He loved to have history read aloud to him, storing facts in his retentive memory, sometimes bringing them out later to help win a battle or to exhort his troops to greater efforts. Court secretaries kept detailed histories of his own exploits.

The one-time nomad was a collector of art and rare manuscripts. This was easy enough—he simply stole what caught his fancy. He surrounded himself with musicians, orators, artists, and sculptors, all gleaned from places he had conquered. His crude tastes became refined over the years; he was fond of leather goods, coral, crystal glasses, and goblets decorated with jewels, gold, and silver. He also liked fine fabric of crimson, white, or green, thoroughbred horses, dogs, and beautiful women.

One of his passions was chess; he could checkmate most of the masters of his time. His game was more complicated than the contemporary one, with a board ten squares by eleven, and with such additional pieces as two camels, two giraffes, two sentinels, two war engines, and a Vizier.

One characteristic of this strange, contradictory man was his attention to peacetime improvements: irrigation ditches, canals, roads, better farming methods. Samarkand itself was turned into a model of beauty and luxury with symmetrical gardens as large as parks, and a wide thoroughfare through the city with a double row of shops, vaulted passageways, and galleries along each side.

The riches of the Orient poured in here. There were caravans of elephants with treasure from India (which he invaded in 1398), gold and ostriches from Egypt, coins and tapestries from Byzantium and Spain.

Tartar official of Turkey

But always the Tartar went out again to conquer and slaughter—Mesopotamia, Georgia, India, Syria. By 1402 he had overrun the Turkish Empire. There now was nothing much else in the world Tamerlane wanted but China. He laid plans to take it, but he was seventy-one years old. One stormy January night in 1405 he took to his bed.

"Pray for my soul," he told his weeping wives. "Do not wail or grieve, for lamentation is pointless. No one yet has ever driven death away by weeping. Instead of tearing your clothes and running madly about, beseech God to be merciful to my soul." He died that same night.

Even in his lifetime, some historians say, a little trade trickled along the Silk Road. But now Asia was swallowed up in anarchy. An anti-foreign dynasty had come to power in China. Once again the East was hidden from the West, known only through the journals of Polo and the friars. The Silk Road was closed to silk forever. Europe turned its face to the West and a new world.

Sericulture had by this time become widespread. It was practiced in Greece, Spain, Sicily, Cyprus, and France. The city of Lyons in France became the industry's European capital. The silk produced by China was still far superior, however. In the second half of the nineteenth century, Europe was importing about 50 percent of the raw product from the Orient by sea.

But by the dawn of the twentieth century much of China's silken glory was gone. That nation had failed to keep pace with the times. In a vain attempt to

The Japanese became leading
silk producers in the early part
of the twentieth century.

recover its position, it resorted to child labor, which in
turn gave rise to horrifying abuses and, eventually, re-
form. The chief problem was not labor, however, but
an insidious silkworm disease that wiped out much of
the stock.

Meanwhile the adaptable Japanese had learned sericulture and embraced it with the same tireless enthusiasm
that they have since bestowed on cameras, motorbikes,
and baseball. Japan capitalized on the craze for silk
goods which developed in the 1920s—shirts, lingerie, and
especially stockings. By 1923 Yokohama was the silk
center of the world.

Craftsmen of the Silk Guild reeled silk by hand in the fourteenth century.

Italian methods of sericulture, sixteenth century

Then, as now, the *basic* industry had changed little
over the centuries: the silkworm still spins its shimmering
cocoon which is then unraveled into silken thread. But
the details were changing. Much of the production
emphasis shifted from village family units to factories.
Unraveling became a mechanized process. Incubators
replaced cruder forms of heating. Scientific air-condi-
tioning techniques made it relatively simple to cater to
the habits of the sensitive worm.

Yet even this improved sericulture could not compete
with the upsurge of nylon and other synthetic fabrics
after World War II. They were the product of a revolution in petro-chemical manufacture, which in turn
was partly stimulated by the war. Try though the silk
industry has to revive its market, it appears that silk may
vanish altogether or else become the scarce luxury item
it was more than 2,000 years ago.

For the Road itself, a great wave of nostalgia has
sprung up in our time. The first to rediscover it were
explorers and archaeologists—notably Sven Anders
Hedin and Sir Marc Aurel Stein. Hedin, a Swede, first
went into the Kashgar region in 1890–91 while still in
his twenties. He made many more journeys, the last
in 1927, and left vivid descriptions of the geography and
perils of the Silk Road. One account tells in painful
detail how his party was lost in the Takla Makan, how
camels died and men fell behind one by one, how Hedin
himself struggled on alone to finally lunge out of the
dunes to water and rescue.

Sven Anders Hedin

Stein, a hardy Britisher, brewed oatmeal porridge on
his journeys and carried hens with him so he could have
fresh eggs. He also left copious records and photographs
(entire mule loads of glass photographic plates were in-

cluded in his caravans) which help reconstruct life on the early Road. Both men, and their followers, unearthed many archaeological treasures—the ruins of forgotten towns, artifacts from wayside watchtowers, fragmented records from Chinese military garrisons, an ancient bolt of silk preserved for centuries in the sands.

These pioneer explorers stirred the imagination of dozens more: scientists, writers, and people who were just weary of the humdrum twentieth century. Most of their travels were between World Wars I and II.

Now visitors are not welcome in Communist China, and large segments of the Road are closed. The route is changing beyond recognition, too. In the 1960s a railway was creeping over the first stage of the Silk Road to link with Russian steel at Aktogay. Oil derricks thrust their geometrical shapes into the sky at Yumen. Refineries hiss and rumble at Lanchow.

Yet in a way the Silk Road is still at the core of history. In June, 1967, a terrible blast drowned out the echoes of camel bells and ghostly voices near the atomic research center of Lop Nor in the Sinkiang province, that desolate stretch of the Silk Road which travelers used to fear most. It was China's sixth nuclear explosion—an H-bomb with a force equal to the bomb that destroyed Hiroshima. The unprecedented exchange of commerce and knowledge over the Silk Road, which saw gunpowder travel from China to the West, has now seen the process reversed. The Silk Road has come full circle.

BIBLIOGRAPHY

Asimov, Isaac, *The Roman Republic*. Boston: Houghton Mifflin Company, 1966.

Collier's Encyclopedia. New York: Crowell Collier & Macmillan, Inc., 1966.

Encyclopedia Britannica. Chicago: Encyclopaedia Britannica, Inc., 1966.

Heichelheim, Fritz M., and Cedric A. Yeo, *A History of the Roman People*. Englewood Cliffs, N. J.: Prentice-Hall, Inc., 1962.

Jones, A. H. M., *The Later Roman Empire* (2 vols.). Norman, Okla.: University of Oklahoma Press, 1964.

Lamb, Harold, *Genghis Khan*. New York: Doubleday & Company, Inc., 1952.

Olschki, Leonardo, *Marco Polo's Asia*. Tr. by John Scott. Berkeley, Calif.: University of California Press, 1960.

Plutarch, "Life of Crassus," *Lives of the Noble Romans*. Abridged edition ed. by Edmund Fuller. New York: Dell Publishing Company, Inc.

Polo, Marco, *Travels*. New York: Grossman Publishers, Inc., 1958.

Reischauer, Edwin O., and John K. Fairbank, *East Asia: The Great Tradition*. Boston: Houghton Mifflin Company, 1958.

Shor, Jean Bowie, *After You, Marco Polo*. New York: McGraw-Hill Book Company, 1955.

INDEX